M000202933

The Pathway to Love

*The most profound way to know yourself
is through the eyes and soul of another*

Contents

Part Three: Love and Transformation

Acknowledgments

I have been in the helping profession for 24 years, and while I have been cultivating this book for many of those years, I believe that now is the right time for me to write it. The culmination of my personal and professional experiences is such that I feel my thoughts on the topic of this book have matured and are ready to be presented.

As with any significant undertaking, I could not have done this alone. Many people along the way have encouraged, believed in, and supported me. It would be impossible for me to name them all, as there have been so many who have touched my life and played a role in who I am and where I am today. However, I would be remiss if I didn't thank the following people who have directly impacted the birth of this book, its accompanying workbook, and *The Pathway to Love* program in its entirety.

First, I would like to thank my wonderful friends and colleagues from "Gerry's Group": Jane Holcomb, Josef Klaus, Leslie Robin, Peri Levin, and Farnaz Tabaee. It was in this group (officially started from a workshop facilitated by Gerry Foster, and thus the group's name) that *The Pathway to Love* was conceived and born. Your support and encouragement kept me moving forward, even during times of self-doubt. Second, I want to thank all my wonderful "readers," whom I am grateful to call my friends: Anita Varisco, Jackie Mills, Peggy Parskey, Michelle Winkley, Karen Holt, Nadine Winter, and Christine Zack. Your thoughtful and honest feedback was crucial to my growth as a writer and the fine-tuning of this manuscript. Third, I want to thank my editor, Marian Pierce, for making the editing process painless and fun, and Bruce Williams and Louise Langerud for their keen proofreading of my work. I am also grateful to Isabelle Ruen (and Starr) for contributing her talent in photography, Ellen Reid for her good counsel, and Sharon Goldinger from PeopleSpeak for generously spending time advising me along the way and always being available to give me helpful hints. Mayapriya Long's vast experience in book design along with Leslie

Robin's lovely interior artwork brought so much warmth and beauty to the book's look and feel. So many others shared their expertise and knowledge as I learned to navigate the publishing world. Please forgive me if I have not specifically named you and know how much I appreciate your support, talent, and advice.

In closing, I dedicate this book to all the people who have entered and touched my life. You have all taught me life lessons, shown me myself, and illuminated my journey. A special message of love goes to my daughters, Nicole and Tanya, who have been my greatest teachers in understanding unconditional acceptance and love.

PART ONE

Creating an Opening

To gain understanding, listen to what others have to say with an open and empty mind, as if you have never heard anything like it before.

Introduction

Remember the feelings of excitement and anticipation the first time you fell in love? Perhaps your first love turned into something meaningful and magical or perhaps into your first heartbreak, but regardless of the outcome, you probably muddled through without much guidance. There is no road map to follow in relationships. We have had various role models to follow, both good and bad, or Hollywood endings to emulate, but we still struggle to navigate our relationships.

The Pathway to Love explores how relationships grow from two strangers coming together to two people creating intimacy, love, and meaning for each other. This developmental approach to understanding relationships is designed to create a structure from which to understand how you impact your relationships and how your relationships impact you. Relationships are about self-responsibility and self-discovery. They provide the perfect mirror into ourselves as well as the opportunity to grow and heal. They are worth protecting and nourishing. In this book, you will learn how to serve the needs of your relationships so that your relationships can naturally support both you and your significant others.

For many years I have worked with people on relationships and have witnessed the various ways they approach them. Most people view their relationships from the perspective of how the other person does or doesn't meet their needs. For example, when I ask people to describe their relationships, they typically describe how the other person treats them or makes them feel. If someone asked you to describe your relationship, what would you say? Would you describe your significant other as someone who supports, loves, accepts, criticizes, encourages, discourages, helps, demands, ignores, understands, rejects, controls, or hurts you?

We tend to focus a lot of energy on how our partner treats us and makes us feel and, in doing so, either idealize or criminalize our partner accordingly, depending on the moment or circumstance at hand. We focus less on understanding how we can nurture our relationship and how our relationship impacts us. When I ask couples to talk about their relationships, they often say that relationships are a lot of work and that they cause stress, drama, pain, obligations, and burdens. I believe the time has come for a paradigm shift. There is a different way to approach relationships and how we relate to others.

I propose we begin to see relationships as mirrors into ourselves, access to true freedom, openings for new possibilities, and catalysts for healing and transformation. From this perspective, the people in our lives have value, regardless of how the relationship met or didn't meet our expectations, hopes, and desires. Our relationships are defined as opportunities rather than expectations that have to be fulfilled. This book outlines the basic tasks, issues, and opportunities that exist as relationships develop and deepen over time, as well as ways to navigate through and among the four phases of the developing relationship.

I decided to write this book for these reasons:

We need each other. We are social beings that depend upon each other for many things: companionship, safety, practical help, problem solving, love, affection, sex, fun, and spiritual needs. We simply cannot survive without each other. And while I understand that our primitive *survival of the fittest* instincts are still alive and well, relating to each other from this perspective alone does not work in our favor. We need to work together in order to ensure that everyone's needs get met. We can all flourish when we adopt a both/and approach as opposed to either/or when it comes to problem solving and relationship building.

Our primal instincts for survival naturally lend themselves to competing with others. Competition works *against* us when there are winners and losers, haves and have-nots, and right and wrong thinking. Competition works *for* us when we use it to come up with an idea or solution that is better than what we had before. It is healthy when it promotes an environment of creativity, synergy, and effective problem solving. In this context, competition creates progress, innovation, and solutions that benefit everyone. Relationships then move toward becoming win-win as opposed to win-lose. Our world becomes a better place and we are better because of this.

The time has come to approach our interdependence from the standpoint of collaboration and mutual learning. We must cherish our relationships, as if they were sacred and fragile beings that deserve being nurtured and protected. It is through our relationships that we find ourselves, our humanity, and our future.

We learn about ourselves through others. The best avenue for self-discovery and self-growth is through the people in our lives. They mirror back to us the qualities about ourselves that we admire and like as well as the qualities about ourselves that we dislike or prefer to deny.

Most significant events in our lives involve people. When those encounters are positive, we learn something new or reaffirm a belief that restores our faith in others and in ourselves. Everything is right in our world. Our confidence grows seamlessly.

When those encounters are negative, we enter the world of conflict. We initiate all our defense mechanisms. We deny, numb, escape, project, and rationalize away all the things that are too painful for us to face—things about ourselves, about others, and about our past. Suddenly, our confidence is compromised. Our world is threatened. We work hard to restore our sense of safety. We yearn to stay still and hidden. We resist the very opportunity that conflict provides—*growth and self-discovery.*

Conflict has acquired a bad reputation.[1] While certain types of conflict can be destructive, constructive conflict is quite good. It allows us to grow and learn. It enables us to engage in creative problem solving. It provides us with a necessary mirror into ourselves. We just need to redefine our relationship to conflict and understand the difference between destructive and constructive conflict. Remember that every time you react to someone, there is an opportunity to learn, understand, and see something about yourself and others. This idea is at the heart of each phase in the developing relationship.

We need to love and be loved. We need love for our emotional well-being just as much as we need water, oxygen, and food for our physical health. And while there are many ways to have love in our lives, for example, by caring for pets, being in nature, or making art, people provide the greatest opportunity for spiritual, emotional, intellectual, and physical connection. This is

---

1. Conflict can be constructive or destructive. Destructive conflict serves to attack the person who holds the opposing view or need until that person "surrenders" or acquiesces to the other's position. Constructive conflict serves to examine the task or issue at hand until a resolution is found that is satisfactory to both parties.

because human beings share the ability to communicate with one another through language and a common culture, history, and biology.

Just as others provide a mirror into ourselves, we do the same for them. We have the power to reflect information in ways that promote either defensiveness or growth. The most powerful context in which to mirror one another is with love. When we truly listen, understand, and accept another, we *create* love. When we are truly heard, understood, and accepted by another, we *experience* love. Where there is love, anything and everything becomes possible.

Most people struggle to create love and intimacy. Although we may have read or heard ideas on how to create love and intimacy, we need to be reminded again and again. We are able to take in information and implement it in different ways at different times throughout our lives. We are forever a work in progress. That is why it is so valuable to hear ideas repeated through different voices in different ways, at different times. This book and accompanying workbook will present you with a specific process designed to create love and intimacy.

Lastly, I am dedicated to creating a world in which people are committed to each other's well-being. In the United States, there is a "me" culture. The individual is valued more than the group. Competition and winning are valued regardless of the costs. Profit comes before people. More is better. Materialism is at an all-time high. We are addicted to constant stimulation and instant gratification, and have created a consumer-driven market that feeds and strengthens this addiction.

When we're not spending money to avoid our own emptiness and failings, we blame ourselves or others when things go wrong. This only results in less connection, more emptiness and deeper despair. We desperately want to feel better and in the pursuit of so-called happiness, spend enormous amounts of money on quick fixes and empty promises. We have a million products promising us everlasting personal happiness and gratification. Where we are falling short (collectively, not necessarily individually) is in making a commitment to the well-being of each other and to the community as a *whole*.

In summary, *The Pathway to Love* provides a developmental approach to and understanding of relationships that will empower you to create the relationship you want with others. As relationships develop, so do the purposes we wish them to fulfill. In the beginning, we first seek to get our own needs met. As our bond and attachment grows, we become more committed to meeting our significant other's needs. But as the relationship itself develops a deeper meaning and purpose, we become committed to making choices and taking actions that support the relationship's needs rather than our own. We treat our relationship as if it were a living, breathing being. When this level of commitment and attentiveness is reached, profound transformation on an individual, relationship, and communal level becomes possible.

My intention is to provide you with the opportunity to grow and thrive within the context of human relationships and community, where you can experience love and authenticity, be seen, heard, understood, and accepted, and do the same unto others.

Who Am I to Say It's So?

I have been working as a licensed psychotherapist for over 20 years, and have master's degrees in both social work and organizational leadership. The concepts presented in the forthcoming chapters on the developmental phases of relationships come from that expertise and experience. However, I don't necessarily want you to accept (or reject) the ideas presented as absolute truths. I would rather you consider the information you read as one of many possible *points of view.* And this is why:

Relationships are complex. There are a multitude of factors playing out in each and every moment, including biological differences, childhood experiences, family of origin, cultural background, psychological constructs, hormonal differences, interpersonal dynamics, past trauma, age, life experiences, and for some who subscribe to metaphysical beliefs, astrological and past life influences. I chose to write this book about the developmental phases of relationships because it provides a framework from which to explore many aspects of ourselves and the dynamics that impact our relationships with others. It is not meant to tackle the entire conversation about relationships, but rather to be one point of entry into that discussion. It is one lens from which to observe ourselves more objectively. It attempts to simplify things enough so that we can see ourselves in the stories that follow. This will create awareness, awareness creates openings, and openings create possibilities—to appreciate, support, and understand one another more profoundly.

As with all points of view, mine should not be taken as an absolute truth. In reality, we don't have absolute truths. We only have a perspective that's based on our current body of knowledge, beliefs, interpretations, and observations. Our body of knowledge changes all the time. Scientists are always discovering new information about our bodies, ecosystems, solar system, and the universe. Things we once believed as "facts," we now refer to as "myths." For example, the world was once believed to be flat. My guess is that when this was proven wrong, some people were able to change their beliefs and understanding regarding the earth's shape and orbit quickly and easily, while others were not. Even when we are confronted with new information, it is challenging to change our beliefs.

Our beliefs are very powerful. They form our identities, and are at the core of how we navigate our relationships. They dictate our behaviors and look for things that reinforce their legitimacy and existence. We all think that our beliefs represent how things really are, when in fact they are simply points of view that developed long ago. Over the course of our lives, we perceive, interpret, and integrate life experiences and observations. Our brain orchestrates this complex process, resulting in what we refer to as "our truths."

For example, person A may believe that the world is a dangerous place, not to be trusted. This "truth" or belief came about because this person grew up in a neighborhood with a lot of violence and crime. Person B, on the other hand, grew up in a protected and safe environment and believes that the world is relatively safe. You can begin to imagine how person A and person B would interpret and react to various situations. The same scenario (let's say seeing three police cars racing by with their sirens on) would probably elicit two very different reactions, both of which would be equally valid based on what we know about person A and person B. From this perspective, you begin to understand that neither one grasps the real "truth" because that person's truth is not an absolute; the world is both safe and dangerous depending on where you stand, who you are, and what is occurring. They are simply examples of two *points of view.*

In relationships, conflict arises from two different *points of view.* I have worked many times with couples that would fight to the death (figuratively speaking) over whose point of view was correct. I would hate to see you get caught in the same trap while reading this book. So here's what I suggest. Don't spend your time and energy deciding if I'm right or wrong in my presentation of ideas because I'm neither. I'm presenting a *point of view* in hopes that it will stimulate, empower, and enlighten you. If you find yourself trying to decide who is right and who is wrong in the stories that follow, try to catch yourself and redirect your thoughts to questions such as "How does their story relate to me? What can I learn?

How can I use this story to help nurture myself, my partner, and our relationship?" That is the power that comes from *points of view* rather than *absolute truths*.

Just as relationships mirror things about ourselves, this book will act as a mirror as well. It will mirror just how wonderful and valuable a human being you are. It will mirror the times, places, and people with whom you've traveled the phases of the developing relationship. It will mirror your successes and failures, your wisdom and blind spots, your blessings and losses. And, finally, it will mirror your deep capacity for love. I appreciate your time and attention in considering this *point of view*, and wish you safe travels as you begin this journey of exploring relationships, love, and self-discovery.

The Four Phases of the Developing Relationship

For the sake of simplifying complexity, I have organized the development of a relationship into four phases. Each phase has certain issues that surface. In addition, each phase has specific tasks that need to be accomplished. While it is implied that once the tasks are mastered and the issues resolved, one will move from phase one to phase two and so on, in reality this is not how it works. There will be a thorough discussion on how developmental theories work in the next section. But in the meantime, keep in mind the following as you begin to learn what each phase offers:

1. You can work on issues in different phases at the same time.

2. Relationships continuously jump back and forth from one phase to another.

3. Sometimes there is overlap; the same or similar issues are present in more than one phase.

Phase One: *Object–Fantasy*

All relationships have a beginning. Everyone who has entered our lives did so as a stranger, someone we met for the first time. It is in this moment that we begin the first phase of the developing relationship. During this phase, several things occur. The person that we just met is really not a person to us at all. We don't know that person. We only know the persona or mask others want to present, and the rest is all up to us. We project ourselves onto them, others onto them, our needs onto them, and our past onto them. People can be idealized or criminalized depending on the circumstances at hand; we simply see what we want or need to see. This first phase is thus aptly named the object-fantasy phase.

In romantic relationships, this phase can easily trick you. Because there may be hormones pumping and fantasies jumping, you feel that you truly know the person you recently met. You may even think you care about them. You may even declare you are in love. However, you cannot possibly know someone that you met just hours, days, or even weeks earlier. It takes time to get to know someone. It takes shared experiences and open, honest communication. In the beginning, you only know and care about that which you have projected onto the other. The other, at this point in time, cannot be seen for who she truly is; this person is there to meet a need, your need; and you will deny your projections and distortions wholeheartedly, for they feel so real.

You do not present your true self either; you collude with the object-fantasy. Just as you cannot possibly know who the other truly is, the other cannot possibly know you. Just as you are projecting onto him, he is projecting onto you. It is a reciprocal dance that creates a synergy we call relationships.

As phase one continues, a lot of anxiety gets activated and acted out. Once you have projected your fantasies about what you want or fear onto the new relationship, you become attached and committed to either making sure the fantasy comes true or making sure your worst fears don't. People are very reactive during this phase. You may find yourself distancing from the other or pursuing the other. You may see the other as perfect and the answer to your prayers or as nothing but potential pain and disappointment.

Because this phase triggers so many issues, it is difficult to differentiate between what's real and what isn't. You have many blind spots at this juncture, both in terms of you and your reactions, as well as those of the other person. It is difficult to see the red flags, let alone act accordingly. Wants, needs, and fantasies take hold. Fears and old wounds run the show. Your actions and reactions are primarily based on these unconscious thoughts and memories. This can result in attaching too quickly or retreating too quickly. This phase challenges you to contain your anxieties, release your attachment to the outcome, understand your fears and desires, and stay present to what is.

While this all may sound daunting, phase one is a wild ride. It's the time when we feel alive and full of anticipation. Anything and everything becomes possible.

Just remember that phase two is coming up.

Phase Two: *Self-Discovery*

Phase one will persist until the object-fantasy projections loosen their grip. Once they do, you begin to see the other person for who she truly is. You begin to reveal yourself for who you truly are. It becomes too difficult to sustain the façade. Warts and all are exposed. In turn, the fantasy about who you want and need the other to be is overpowered by behaviors and truths that can no longer be ignored or suppressed. You begin to react to who the person really is, rather than who you wish she was. Fantasies are lost, disappointments surface, and the real work of relationships begins.

While on the one hand, projections begin to fade, on the other, projections begin to intensify. You are challenged with looking into the mirror that another provides. You must deal with all the reactivity and intensity that correlates with losing the object-fantasy as well as what you continue to project onto the other. You must begin to deal with yourself and your significant other in honest and authentic ways. In so doing, you begin to distinguish her stuff from yours. This is no easy task but one that requires consciousness of behaviors, insight, and the ability to accept yourself without judgment. It requires letting go of the need to be right and being willing to listen to the other with the intent to understand.

The gifts that are yours for the taking in phase two are self-discovery, self-love, and love of another. You begin to understand yourself in a way that results in real power and choice. Your decisions and actions in life are no longer made in reaction to the past or imagined threats. You are able to make choices from a place of power. You discover that your personal integrity and self-care are more important than anything else. You learn what self-love is. Lastly, by making yourself available to understand another for who he truly is, you allow yourself to experience real love, not love based on fantasy and projection.

As you move through phase two, you will find out that your significant other is not as perfect or as threatening as you once thought. In dealing with this disappointment or relief, you have the opportunity to learn more about yourself. You learn how tolerant or intolerant you are to certain qualities and behaviors. You become aware of your beliefs and how they affect your interpretations and reactions to others. You are reminded of your own vulnerabilities and sensitivities. Finally, you have the opportunity to be more compassionate and empathic with yourself and others.

Phase two encourages you to reassess what is truly important to you and what is not. This is the time to put aside your projections and really get to know and understand your significant other. Listening skills are tested, assumptions are challenged, and an attachment develops that is based more in reality and anchored in love. There is a lot to do in phase two. It is a time to discover new things about yourself. You will be reminded, once again, how your past is still running your life and with this awareness, you become more able to create with your partner an intimate relationship that works.

It is not easy to acknowledge things we may not necessarily like about ourselves and the people we love. It takes courage. Only when we are able to be fully present with what is are we able to accept what is and grow. At the same time, it is important that we celebrate those qualities about one another that make our relationships special. This is when our relationships begin to take shape and form. They become real.

From here, it's only one small step toward phase three.

Phase Three: *Personal Transformation*

While phase two enlightens you to reveal your true self, phase three asks you to accept your significant other for who he truly is. This means that you accept their personal truths, points of view, and choices without manipulating and controlling the outcome. In turn, you take full responsibility for yourself, including your feelings, thoughts, and actions, without blaming the other. You and your partner genuinely support each other in your respective journeys.

This occurs through honest and authentic communication. Instead of being caught in the midst of reactivity, you are able to appreciate and learn from the mirroring that takes place between the two of you. You recognize that the mirroring never really ends and that there is value in learning about yourself through your interactions and reactions to each other.

As you traverse the terrain of phase three, you become a skilled communicator. You learn to catch any reactivity and process what you need to know about yourself before responding. You ask questions in order to test your understandings and assumptions. You are able to communicate your needs and wants as requests rather than demands or silent wishes. You no longer see conflicts as an opening to prove the other wrong. Alternatively, conflicts are a vehicle toward deeper understanding, acceptance, and love. You and your partner are able to be vulnerable and authentic, thus creating genuine intimacy. You are now totally committed to each other's well-being.

Phase three requires you to continuously self-reflect while managing your reactivity. It necessitates integrity and honest communication at all times. It is not easy to accept someone or something as is. Our nature is designed to control and manipulate (actively or passively) so we can have things "our way." It takes maturity and patience to approach communicating and getting your needs met in a different way. You need to be willing to be disappointed and experience loss. Sometimes this includes making difficult choices and creating new beliefs.

The gift that's available in phase three is personal transformation. The ability to be with what is, to be present, generates an opening. Genuine acceptance and love creates a space for new ways of being and living. Experiencing deep and profound love becomes possible. You and your significant other can soar to higher levels of consciousness, experiencing peace and expansiveness in your daily lives.

Once you move successfully through phase three, you arrive at phase four.

Phase Four: *Relational Transformation*

While phase three supports personal transformation, phase four supports relational transformation. This means that the relationship goes beyond simply meeting the needs of both individuals. A shared purpose and meaning (vision) is created or emerges. Each person in the relationship supports each other in working toward that purpose. In other words, each person lives into the vision. The whole becomes greater than the sum of its parts and the well-being of the relationship is equally important as, if not more important than, the well-being of each individual. The relationship becomes a living, breathing entity in and of itself.

This transformation is accomplished by engaging in deeper dialogues about what the relationship needs in order to flourish. Authentic and open communication occurs at a deeper level. Even deeper levels of love and commitment are felt. The transformation not only occurs on an individual level, as in phase three, but also on a relationship level. This can't help but have an impact on those around you. As your actions and choices support your vision, those same actions and choices will inform all areas of your life. Your relationship not only makes a difference for you both but also will affect other people in your lives. The power of love and transformation is that profound.

Phase four is a unique phase in the development of a relationship. We define and redefine the purpose and meaning of our relationships throughout our lifetimes. Our definitions usually have a more transactional or practical purpose, for example, our relationship supports our ability to run a household. We are together to raise and nurture our children and family members, or our relationship supports each of us so that we can succeed in our careers. The purpose and meaning sometimes extends to the greater community, for example, our relationship provides resources to important causes in the pursuit of making a difference in the world.

As your relationship deepens, the meaning and purpose often begin to take on a different feel. You start to ascribe attributes and meaning to your relationship as if it were a person, a separate entity with a personality all its own. For example, your purpose and meaning might include attributes such as peaceful and easygoing, fun and adventurous, sensitive and compassionate, supportive and intimate, dream fulfilling, growing and transforming. You create a vision for where you want your relationship to go and what that would look like. At this point, all your decisions and actions are in alignment with your vision. You understand that if you do something that is not good for the relationship, it will not be good for you or your partner.[1] You support the relationship in being all that it can be rather than solely supporting yourselves as individuals. In so doing, you and your partner thrive. Your relationship thrives. The world around you thrives.

---

1. Whereas the opposite does not work the same way—that is, you can do something that will be good for you, but not for the relationship.

It's not easy to make decisions that are in the best interests of the relationship rather than yourself. We are ego-centric by nature. It's difficult to trust and know that when you act in alignment with the relationship's needs, everyone wins in the end. It may not look exactly the way you thought or intended. You may instead find the unexpected. This is where the magic lives. You may find yourself living a life you never thought imaginable. Be open to how life unfolds. Be open to the mystery and the uncertainty. There will always be bumps along the way, but if you keep your eye on your vision, you will find your way through with more ease and grace.

Phase four is where my vision comes to life—you are a full participant in creating a global community in which we are all committed to each other's well-being. The well-being of ALL human beings becomes the vision that we live into.

Understanding How Developmental Processes Work

You are about to hear the stories of four couples.[1] Each couple is in a different phase of their relationship dealing with different sets of circumstances. I've captured a moment in time in each couple's lives that reflects the particular phase presented. My objective is to provide you the opportunity to see how the four phases of a developing relationship translate from theory to real life. However, as you read these stories, it is important to remember a few things about developmental theories.

---

1. All characters and stories appearing in this work are fictitious. Any resemblance to real persons, living or dead, is purely coincidental.

Development Never Takes an Absolutely Linear Path

While developmental theories imply that you will follow a linear progression, that is, you will move from the first phase to the second, then the third and so on, in reality people and couples move in and out of phases all the time. Just because you've progressed from phase two to three doesn't mean that you will never revisit phase one or two again. In fact, it is entirely possible to live in more than one phase at a time.

Think about the development of a person. Just because you've moved from childhood to adolescence to adulthood doesn't mean the child in you disappears. You may be an adult but will sometimes be triggered in a way that takes you back to feelings and behaviors you had in younger phases of development. We all find ourselves in situations that take us back to another time and place, forcing us to revisit old issues and old ways of being. Just think back on the last holiday dinner you had with your family. During family gatherings, many people find themselves reacting in the same manner that they did when they were children. All of a sudden, the confident, competent adult turns into the "baby of the family." Sibling rivalries get reactivated. The environment and situation in which you find yourself has a lot to do with which development tasks reappear. In addition, as you prepare to grow and shift developmentally, you will temporarily regress to prepare for the developmental leap.

So be prepared. As an adult, you bounce back and forth between developmental tasks all the time. Sometimes you will be dealing with individuation and separation issues that are heightened in adolescence, while at other times you will be dealing with attachment issues that occur during infancy. Sometimes you will be dealing with crises that require you to address many developmental tasks from different stages all at the same time. In fact, the greater the amount of stress and the more severe the crisis, the higher the likelihood your behaviors will be regressive, at least initially.

The same goes for relationships. While there is a natural and necessary developmental process to traverse, you will need to address all four phases throughout the lifetime of the relationship. You never completely master any one phase. This is an ongoing process. Relationships continuingly challenge you to grow and evolve. The goal is to become proficient in identifying what issues from which phase are presenting themselves and how best to respond. In doing so, your skill set and emotional maturity will continue to expand as you resolve (and re-resolve) the issues and successfully navigate the developmental phases.

There Are No Clear Timelines to Follow

Most people like to know how long it will take to *get there*. While I would love to give you the magic formula, none exists. People move through the phases in their own time frames. Each person and each relationship is unique. Some people are well guarded and defended, while others are more open and easily attach. Some people will wear their hearts on their sleeves, while others will carefully reveal themselves methodically over a long period of time. How you are with one partner may look different than how you are with another. In other words, there is no way to know exactly how your relationship will unfold. Furthermore, there is no *right* way or timeline; there is only *your* way and timeline. That timeline need not be rushed. There are important things to experience and learn about yourself and your significant other in each phase of development. There are obstacles to remove, defenses to let down, and experiences to share. All this takes time, trust, courage, and commitment. Don't ever feel like you need to compare your journey to anyone else's.

There are many factors that impact how quickly people move from one phase to another. These include individual differences, how often you see each other, the quality of your interactions and communications, what experiences you have together, what other circumstances are occurring in your respective lives, and so on. Remember, you are two unique individuals participating in the dance. This creates dynamics that either impinge or propel the speed in which you move through the phases. For example, two people who are afraid of intimacy will spend more time in phases one and two, whereas two people who know and understand themselves fairly well will most likely move more quickly toward phases two and three.

Other circumstances can impact the developmental pace. If a couple experiences a crisis together, they will have the opportunity to move forward more quickly because crises tend to break down defense mechanisms, creating openings for authenticity and connection. All the unique sets of circumstances and personalities at hand will play into how the relationship develops and in what time frame. Remember, there is no right way or right timing to move through a developing relationship.

This leads me to my final comment.

The Choice Is Yours

Every person and every couple has free choice in the matter. There is no perfect way to navigate relationships. Long-term relationships require effort and commitment to keep them healthy and growing. How, when, and if you choose to move through any one phase is your choice. There are no shortcuts and no hard and fast rules. Many people choose not to have intimate relationships. Some people choose to stay in one phase and go no further. Other people would like to have a relationship that moves through all four phases and don't know how to get there. Wherever you are on the continuum is just fine. It's far better to accept where you stand and own your choices rather than beat yourself up, make yourself or another wrong, or believe you're a victim.

The more we judge, the more we resist, the more we stay stuck in pain and suffering. It really is that simple. And for many, the choice to have or have not comes from personal values, experiences, and life goals. There is nothing wrong with this choice. So wherever you find yourself standing today, everything is just fine. If you are satisfied with your current relationship (or non-relationship), then all is good. If you are not satisfied, then accept what is not working and determine how you wish to proceed. This book will allow you to take a look at yourself and see what needs to be seen. It will offer a context from which to examine where you currently stand and where to go from here. It will inspire you to see what might be available if you so choose. And finally, it will encourage you to listen, accept, and love more.

Let's begin the journey. We'll start with phase one. I'd like you to meet Sue and Joe.

PART TWO

Four Couples,
Four Stories,
Four Relationships
Unfold

While love is always present and available to us,
it usually takes two hearts, two minds,
and two souls to find our way there.

Phase One:
Object–Fantasy

The Beginning:
When Sue Meets Joe

Sue meets Joe at a conference she attends for human resource managers. She sits next to him in a morning session on coaching managers with difficult employees. She finds Joe to be an attractive, friendly man. They compare notes and opinions about the presenter and subject matter throughout the training session. After the session they decide to have lunch together. During the meal, they discover they have many mutual interests, both personal and professional. They both enjoy working with managers who are having difficulty getting their employees to perform at satisfactory levels. They both enjoy spending time outdoors, walking or bicycling, and prefer these activities to those that require a lot of money or time with crowds. The lunch ends. Since they are going to attend different sessions in the afternoon, they decide to exchange business cards to keep in touch.

Sue drives home excited. She had noticed that Joe didn't wear a wedding ring. While this doesn't conclusively mean he is single and available, Sue decides that he probably isn't married. He was very attentive and seemed interested in what she had to say. She hopes that Joe was interested in her socially as well as professionally. She makes up all kinds of conclusions as to who Joe is in a matter of a few hours. The list includes kind, friendly, smart, physically active, concerned about the environment, attentive, a good listener, very attractive, interested in her, available for a relationship, funny, well-educated, and a lot of fun to be around. While Sue rationally understands that she has just met Joe and doesn't know him well, she's sure that the qualities she saw in him during the time they were together are very real and true. She feels there is a lot of potential and can't help but fantasize about a future with Joe. She waits to see if he'll contact her.

But when Joe doesn't contact her the following week, she begins to worry and feel sad. She feels a sense of loss. While on the one hand, she knows she hasn't known Joe long enough to really *lose* him, she feels a loss nonetheless.

The Beginning: When Joe Meets Sue

Joe notices Sue right away when he enters the training session and purposely sits down next to her. He thinks Sue is very attractive and sexy. As they converse, Joe notices she also has a good sense of humor. She appears to be bright and educated. He also can't help but notice she has great legs as she crosses them back and forth under her skirt. Joe had been dating someone for a short time, but that had ended several weeks before the conference, and he feels there just might be some promise in Sue. Joe decides it is worth pursuing and invites Sue to have lunch with him after the training session. He discovers at lunch that they have some things in common, and that she appears to be attracted to him. She laughs at his jokes, shakes her head in agreement when he shares his ideas on human resources management, and leans toward him when she responds to his questions. She seems to be an independent and secure woman. Joe can't help but fantasize what sex would be like with Sue. He gives her his card after lunch and is pleased when she quickly reciprocates.

On the way home, Joe's thoughts quickly turn toward work and the meeting that is scheduled the next morning with his boss. He wonders what bad news he'll receive. Occasionally, he thinks about Sue. He remembers her smile and the way she brushed her hair away from her face. Her attractiveness is growing on him. Joe's thoughts vacillate between Sue and work as he drives slowly through the rush hour traffic. When he arrives home, he takes Sue's business card out of his pocket and slips it into his wallet.

The next day, Joe meets with his boss. He gets the bad news that the company is downsizing in response to diminishing sales. Joe and the vice president of Human Resources spend the next few hours developing a plan of action. Joe feels overwhelmed. The next few days pass quickly, and although he occasionally fantasizes about getting together with Sue, his primary focus is on work and the horrendous tasks and challenges that lie ahead of him. He has never participated in this kind of downsizing before and feels insecure about how he will handle it. He is also worried about his own job security.

Another week goes by and Joe feels the need to de-stress and decompress. He needs a distraction from what is happening at work. He thinks of Sue and sends her an e-mail.

The Beginning after the Beginning

In the e-mail he asks her if she would be interested in meeting for lunch one day to talk about the conference and how they were implementing the information into their respective human resource departments. Sue quickly agrees to the lunch meeting, and they schedule it for later that week. Lunch goes well. Sue enjoys Joe's sense of humor and the values he demonstrates in how he talks about his work. They share some of their more challenging situations at work (although Joe doesn't talk about the downsizing) and Sue feels supported by Joe as he offers valuable suggestions. They share things about their histories and families, such as, where they were born, are their parents still alive and well, how many siblings they have, and where they went to college. Sue feels her attraction to Joe growing stronger. Joe gives Sue a hug when they part.

Sue's excitement is increasing. She is now very attracted to Joe and begins to fantasize about their first kiss. She anticipates his next communication and is anxious to see him again. She hopes he feels the same, thinks he does, but isn't sure and doesn't want to get her hopes too high. She tells her friends how great Joe is and how he possesses all the qualities that are important to her. She says that she genuinely likes Joe and cares about him a lot, even that she feels a special connection. She starts fantasizing about their future together, imagining trips they will take, when they will move in, even how many children they will have. She creates an entire life with Joe in her mind. And while she reminds herself that she has just met Joe, she can't help but dream of the life she has always wanted.

Joe also enjoys their lunch. Sue continues to laugh at his jokes and makes him feel like he's on top of his game. He likes her flirtatious nature and is feeling an even stronger physical attraction. He leaves lunch believing that it was a good call to send her that e-mail and take a break from the stressors at work. Sue was good company. He sees her as independent, nondemanding, very supportive, and probably good in bed. Once things settle down at work, he plans on calling her and making another date, perhaps dinner at his house.

Let's stop and take a look at what we know:

1. Sue and Joe each believe they know a lot about the other. However, at this point, they only know what they have projected onto each other. They're still both objects upon which they have projected all their fantasies and desires about who they want the other to be. All they really know is what they did or said, didn't do or didn't say. They don't know their respective motivations or intentions. Truth be told, they simply have not spent enough time together to know much at all.

2. Sue has experienced Joe in a certain way. How Joe really is remains unknown. Her interpretations of Joe's actions and words are based on many factors—her wants and

desires, her fantasies and past, her experience with others who behave similarly to Joe, and to some extent, what Joe wants her to know and see. The same goes for Joe with regard to how he experiences Sue.

3. Joe and Sue feel a sexual attraction to each other. They each interpret the attraction differently. Sue sees a special connection between the two of them. Joe thinks Sue will be good in bed. At this point, dopamine, the hormone of attraction, is beginning to surge. Dopamine gives us the feeling of well-being and sexual attraction. It is physiologically driven, not person driven, although certain people will trigger this hormone more than others. This hormone also plays a role in making us believe we know someone more than we do. Joe and Sue don't know that dopamine is affecting their perceptions and judgments.

4. Sue says she cares about Joe, but really she cares about continuing to feel the way she does when she's around him. In turn, Joe

feels good about himself when he's around Sue. He's sure that Sue is the reason he feels so good. And while they may care about each other as fellow human beings, this caring is on a superficial level. They cannot possibly care about each other in a deep and profound way because they have not established any real intimacy. They are still in the throes of phase one.

5. Both Sue and Joe are carefully selecting which aspects of themselves they want to reveal. While Sue may be genuine in her responses, her responses to Joe are colored by her need to look good to him, rather than on how she truly feels. Joe also wants to look good, so in turn he presents himself as charming and together, not wanting Sue to know how stressed out and insecure he's feeling at work.

6. Sue is responding to Joe as if all of her projections were the truth and isn't conscious that she's doing this. Her fantasies and hormones have taken hold. Although she is

somewhat aware that she doesn't know Joe all that well, she is still reacting as if her personal interpretations and projections belong to Joe and not to her.

7. Joe thinks he is relating to Sue as a person, but in actuality, most of his behaviors and thoughts of Sue are sexually driven. He believes that Sue admires him, and this fuels his desire to have sex with her. At this point, Sue may be more of an object designed to make him feel like a man and satisfy his sexual needs rather than a real person who has needs of her own.

8. Lastly, Sue and Joe cannot help but do all of the above. It is a natural and normal phase in the development of relationships.

Welcome to the dance. Phase one has just begun.

Over the next few weeks, Joe and Sue go out on a few more dates. They continue to find each other good company. Sue finds Joe more and more charming and is sure "he's the one." Joe likes how good Sue makes him feel, which he appreciates given how bad things are at work. He still hesitates to share his stressors and insecurities with Sue, instead focusing on doing fun activities and keeping the conversation light. Sue still wants to be seen as independent and easygoing, so she doesn't push for more time with Joe, even though she would like to see him more than once a week. She is enjoying Joe's attention and believes that Joe will eventually spend more time with her as they get closer.

On their fourth date, Joe and Sue make love for the first time. While they're both a little shy their first time in bed, they feel good about being together. Sue feels they have crossed a certain threshold. She feels closer to Joe and is sure that their relationship has been cemented. She wants to take things to the next level, to be able to talk more about their past histories and dreams for the future. But something inside her tells her not to push. She continues to hold back, allowing Joe to set the pace. She decides not to stay the night. Joe gives her a big hug and kiss when she leaves his apartment for home. He tells her he'll call in the morning.

The Beginning of the End:
Sue Reacts to Joe

Sue doesn't hear from Joe the next day and becomes increasingly anxious. Why hasn't he called? She dreams up all kinds of reasons—some about her and others about him. Perhaps he had a family emergency or was called into work unexpectedly. She decides to wait a couple of days to see if he'll call, but by the third day, when her feelings of rejection have increased, she can no longer wait, and does what every woman would tell her *not* to do: she calls him. Sue simply cannot tolerate feeling rejected. She wants to continue to feel the way she has for the past month. They were getting along so well, and she felt so sure that he wanted her in his life. How dare Joe behave in a way that takes that feeling away, replacing it with anxiety and worry that she is not good enough for him!

Joe is happy to hear from Sue. He takes her assertiveness as a compliment. He woke up the morning after they slept together to a phone call from his friend inviting him to a basketball game. He accepted the invitation and forgot about his intentions to call Sue. He had also been very busy throughout the week, although he had planned on calling Sue at some point when he had more free time.

They talk for about 15 minutes and then Joe says he has to get off the phone as he has plans for the evening with friends. He thanks Sue for calling and tells her to have a great week. Sue is not pleased. Her previous positive projections onto Joe have stopped. She now sees him as a hurtful, rejecting, insensitive man who doesn't even have the decency to let her know if he plans on seeing her again or even calling her again for that matter. She controls her urge to call him back and ask him directly what his intentions are. Does he want a relationship with her or not? On some level, she knows that would not be taken well, and on a deeper level, she knows she may be overreacting.

Joe gets off the phone, not thinking twice about Sue and the conversation, and leaves to meet his friends. He still plans on calling Sue later, probably at the end of the week, when work demands have settled down and his schedule isn't as busy. In Joe's mind, all is well. He figures he'll connect with Sue later in the week and will see when they are both available to get together.

Sue, however, is now an emotional wreck.

What Joe doesn't know is that Sue's parents divorced when Sue was four, and her father was an inconsistent presence in her life thereafter. Sue never knew when she would see him again, and often felt dismissed, ignored, unloved, and abandoned. She loved her father and desperately wanted his attention. He was so much fun to be with and made her feel so special. As a child, she was confused. On the one hand he made her feel so good. On the other, he would say one thing and do another. He promised to call and didn't. He promised to take her to the carnival but wouldn't show. Sometimes he'd come through, other times not. Sue never knew if she'd be disappointed or thrilled. It was like playing Russian roulette.

Joe doesn't know that his behaviors in the past few days have triggered an entire world for Sue—a world that was formed many years ago, long before Joe ever sat down next to Sue at that fateful human resource conference. What's more, Sue is not aware that Joe's actions sent her off into another time and place. She is sure she's reacting to Joe, his insensitive behavior and confusing messages, not her father.

She begins to pace around her apartment, feeling hurt, angry, and confused. Once those feelings soften, anxiety sets in. She feels an urgency to reconnect with Joe and get affirmation that he is still interested in her. She begins to think of ways and reasons to contact him. She could send him that article about succession planning that she had mentioned to him during their first lunch date. She could wait several more days and if he doesn't call her by then she could pretend that her phone unintentionally called him and with apologies follow-up with another call. She could call and simply invite him to dinner. Her imagination goes wild, and the ideas continue to flood in. After some thought and calls to friends, she decides to wait two days. If she doesn't hear from him by then, she'll e-mail him the article. Surely he'll respond if only out of courtesy, and based on the type of response she receives, she'll find out more about his intentions.

When Sue doesn't hear from Joe, she implements her plan and sends him the article via e-mail. She intentionally makes it sound casual, as she does not want Joe to know how upset she is. At this point, she just wants to reconnect and be reassured that Joe still cares about her. She anxiously awaits his response, checking her e-mail account compulsively. Sue has worked herself up into a tizzy. She tells herself that she has only known this guy a month or so and if she never hears back from him, so be it. It obviously wasn't meant to be. And yet, she can't understand why he isn't being more attentive. They were together intimately. The least he could do is reassure her that he cares about her and wants to pursue a relationship.

As her feelings escalate, her past drives her assumptions. Her actions are based more on her past relationship with her father than her current relationship with Joe. New and equally powerful projections are taking hold. Joe is no longer her knight in shining armor, but rather someone who is just like her father. She has lost her power. She has given that to Joe (that is, her father). Her well-being, self-esteem, and future happiness are now in his hands.

Joe is of course oblivious to what Sue is experiencing. Joe is simply going about a workweek that is exceptionally demanding and busy as the company prepares to downsize and lay off 15 percent of its workforce. The last thing Joe is thinking about is Sue and her reaction to their last phone call just two days ago. As far as he's concerned, everything is fine between them and he intends to call her soon.

Later that day, Joe reads Sue's e-mail but is so buried in work that he moves on to other more pressing e-mails, thinking he'll read the article and get back to Sue at a later time when he's not feeling so swamped with crises at work. By the time the day has ended, Sue is feeling even more desperate. "Why wouldn't he respond to such a considerate e-mail? What's the matter with this guy?" After some time, she tries to think of reasons why he might not have responded other than the fact that he is rejecting her and wants her out of his life. She wonders if perhaps the e-mail went directly into a junk mail account at work. This plausible explanation calms Sue down, and she decides that if he doesn't e-mail her back by the end of the day, she will call and leave a message asking if he received the e-mail and letting him know she can resend it to another e-mail account if it did not come through. She feels satisfied with this plan, calms down, and is able to focus on other things.

The End of the Beginning

By the end of the workday, Sue still hasn't heard from Joe. She calls his cell phone, hoping that he will not pick up so she can leave an innocent, polite message. Joe is in a meeting at the time, notices her call, but lets his voice mail pick up. He leaves work late, completely drained from all the pressures from the day. When he arrives home, he sits down in front of his television and listens to his voice mails. He hears Sue's message inquiring about the e-mail. Joe feels a little puzzled and somewhat pressured by the communications from Sue. He has an uneasy feeling. He likes Sue and appreciates her thoughtfulness in sending him the article. He had told her that he was interested in reading it, and Sue had remembered that and sent it. And since he hadn't acknowledged that he received the message, it kind of made sense that she had called to find out if he had. Joe feels a little guilty that he hasn't taken the time to acknowledge the e-mail. While things have been crazy at work, it would have taken less than a minute to e-mail Sue, thank her, and possibly even let her know what was going on with him at work. Logically, this all made sense and he knew that her phone call was not a big deal.

But despite this reasoning, Joe is feeling suffocated. Why did she call to ask him whether or not he received the e-mail? It had only been a few hours since he received it. They had spoken just a couple of days ago. Why was she now calling him so often? He wondered if she was expecting him to be with her every day now that they had had sex. He starts to react to Sue as if she were overcontrolling, overbearing, and needy. It also occurs to him that perhaps Sue thought he needed that article, that somehow he was not up to the job at hand and lacked knowledge and skill in this area. He begins to see Sue as the enemy, someone who is going to control him, rather than make him feel like a respected, admired man. He certainly is not going to let her control him. Instead of returning Sue's call, he goes out of his way to delete the message and her number from his cell phone. He wants this crazy person out of his life.

Sue never hears from Joe again.

What Sue doesn't know is that Joe's mother is domineering, controlling, and critical to the point of being psychologically and emotionally abusive. Joe could do nothing right growing up. His mother demeaned him every time he did something "wrong" and tried to control his every move and his every decision, especially those that impacted the way she thought he should be. Joe's mother needed her children, particularly Joe, her only son, to be and act a certain way in order for her to feel loved and worthwhile. Joe grew up feeling responsible for his mother's emotional well-being. She demanded he be there for her when summoned. When he grew up and left home, she told him he needed to call her every day. He knows all too well the consequences for displeasing his mother and showing anything but loyal attention and affection when mandated. Joe unknowingly entered his mother's world when he heard Sue's message. His past deleted Sue's message, not Joe. His relationship with his mother determined the fatal outcome to his emerging relationship with Sue. Joe was no longer in charge.

As time progressed Joe realizes that Sue probably just wanted to be considerate and helpful, not imposing and abusive. He also realizes that Sue was probably just checking to see if he received the e-mail. He is aware that the week she e-mailed was exceptionally stressful and that Sue had not known this. He considers sending her an e-mail explaining this, thanking her for the article, and letting her know he'll call her over the weekend to make plans to get together again.

At the same time, Joe can't shake this horrible feeling that compels him to run as far away from Sue as possible. He still feels deep inside that she is persecuting him, making him wrong for not being responsive to her, and will "chop his head off" when or if he calls her back. Emotionally, he's not able to take the risk. He can't control the strong impulse to break away from Sue and save himself, or at least that's how it feels to him. He's sure that Sue is just like his mother, requiring him to be at her beck and call. He will never allow anyone to smother him again. His mother was more than he could handle. In Joe's mind, his life and sanity are at stake!

So while Joe is aware that he is reacting strongly to Sue's actions, he is unable to manage his reactivity and test reality. He is unwilling to be vulnerable and see if Sue is really like his mother or not. Joe doesn't return Sue's call and never hears from her again.

Let's stop and take a look at what we know:

1. As the relationship develops, Sue begins to feel vulnerable and scared. She is aware that she wants this relationship to work but is unaware that she is trying to control the outcome. In trying to control the outcome, she holds back from being authentic with Joe,

becoming somewhat manipulative instead —that is, sending articles, rather than managing her anxiety or having an honest conversation about her concerns directly with Joe.

2. Both Sue and Joe are now projecting their respective parent onto each other. The positive projections that were present are replaced by negative ones based on fears and past wounds. The two react to each other as if they were their parents, not Sue and Joe. Their reactivity happens in isolation. Neither one knows what is going on; only the impact from their behaviors and choices are felt.

3. From an objective perspective, neither Sue nor Joe may be anything like their respective parent. Sue and Joe still don't know each other well enough and long enough to understand the motives and intentions behind their behaviors. The opportunity to understand themselves and the other was lost. The possibility of having a relationship

different from that with their parent will never actualize.

4. The attachment between Sue and Joe was not strong enough to overcome the situation. The projections took over. The objects remain objects. Nothing was gained. No new learning took place. Joe and Sue only reinforced their beliefs formed in childhood. Women want to consume, annihilate, and control you; men will reject, abandon, and dismiss you.

The End of the Beginning: The Aftermath of Sue and Joe

Sue feels hurt and angry that Joe never returns her call or e-mail. Her pride and ego prevent her from reaching out again. She will not give Joe another chance to hurt her. She doesn't understand why Joe rejected her when they had such a great time together. She thought there were real feelings between them. She cannot fathom what she did wrong. And while she logically knows she is still a good person, she can't help but wonder if she is simply unlovable. She is left feeling resigned and disappointed in herself, disappointed in Joe, and disappointed with life. She wonders if she'll ever have the relationship she desires and is beginning to doubt whether she will. She feels destined to live out her past. Deep down she believes all men are like her dad. Unless she is able to confront her beliefs, this won't change.

Joe feels angry and guilty. He is angry that another woman he liked and was attracted to ended up being controlling, needy, and suffocating. He feels guilty for not returning Sue's call. On some level he knew she didn't do anything to deserve his reaction. He feels guilty that he had not done what he had learned to do as a small boy—to take care of another's emotional well-being. He imagined that Sue was feeling hurt and angry because of him.

However, Joe also feels relieved. He knows he has a habit of ending relationships early and abruptly. But in the end, he has escaped suffocation and persecution. He feels safe. He feels back in control of his life, ensuring that no other woman will control him the way his mother does. If only he could do the same with his mother. How he wishes he could cut her off as easily, but he can't. He is still imprisoned by her. Even when his mother dies, nothing will change. His mother and their relationship are now a part of him. Joe understands this and in some way has accepted his fate. The only thing left for him to do is to keep moving forward with vigilance.

The End of Phase One

Sue and Joe began their relationship with positive projections. They liked what they saw in each other and liked the way they felt. Their attraction to each other continued to build as their levels of dopamine and testosterone rose. If they had stayed that course, they could have remained in phase one for a long time. Doing so would have enabled them to attach to each other sufficiently so that when the object-fantasies began to fade, they could begin the work of phase two.

At some point in any relationship, issues get triggered. In this case, both Sue's and Joe's past buttons got triggered early. Sue became anxious quickly. While she tried to manage her anxieties, she did so with only partial success. Joe succumbed to his core fears and beliefs.

He was unable to manage his reactivity in a way that would enable him to test reality, take ownership of his projections, and begin to understand Sue for who she truly was. Instead, his projections onto Sue contributed to the demise of the relationship.

Sue and Joe are a perfect example of how projections can quickly go from good to bad. If one does not understand the developmental tasks at hand, it is easy to act as if one is relating to the other as a person and not an object on which to project. Phase one, when people are still objects and not real people, is a make or break time. You can easily attach yourself with a positive projection or detach yourself with a negative one. Sometimes the two people involved will vacillate between the two, thus the on-again, off-again, chaotic new relationship syndrome.

Phase one looks different in every relationship. You may find yourself traversing phase one with joy, with pain, or a bit of both. This will depend on what types of projections are playing out for each individual involved and how they mix together. There are many possible dance steps from which to choose in phase one.

Lastly, there is no right way to move through phase one. Some couples stay there indefinitely, vacillating between positive and negative projections. Some couples move on to phase two in a relatively short amount of time. Others bounce back and forth between phases one and two. And, of course, some relationships end here, like Joe and Sue's.

In summary, phase one is really about

- Relating to the other as an object even though you believe otherwise
- Projecting positive or negative qualities, traits, and feelings onto the other (which may or may not be true)
- Getting triggered, positively or negatively, often unconsciously
- Getting anxious about what will happen next
- Having fantasies about what will happen next
- Trying to control what will happen next
- Holding on to the fantasy and avoiding loss
- Feeling the effects of dopamine, thus feeling in love or at least in lust
- Attaching and detaching

You know you're leaving phase one and entering phase two when you start to self-reflect. You begin to take responsibility for your reactions. Once sure that you knew who your significant other was, you begin to see that your perceptions were skewed. You are now willing to consider other possible truths, both about yourself and your partner. It is a hard (or soft) landing into reality.

Let's take a look at phase two through the eyes of Angela and John.

Phase Two:
Self-Discovery

The Story of Angela and John

Angela and John have been dating for six months. They are both divorced and have children ranging from 10 to 18 years of age. Angela and John have enjoyed their time together. They have intentionally kept their relationship between themselves, wanting to make sure that it was going somewhere before bringing their children into the picture. They see each other about once a week for dinner and every other weekend when they don't have their kids. They have been able to negotiate how much time they spend together and how they spend that time fairly easily. For the most part, they have had positive projections, seeing each other as easygoing, fun, and flexible.

Things start to change on one beautiful fall day. John was finding it increasingly difficult to convince his teenage children to spend time with him and was feeling the pressure of connecting with them before they left for college. However, on this day, John's 15-year-old daughter, Janine, has agreed to spend the day with him, and they are trying to decide what to do. Janine suggests shopping and a movie. John tries to envision sitting alone while his daughter tries on clothes and finds it difficult to muster up any enthusiasm. He thinks how nice it would be to have Angela along. Janine would have a woman's perspective on fashion. He pictures the three of them together and asks Janine how she would feel if he invited Angela to come along. Janine says, "It's about time I meet her. You've been dating awhile now."

John starts to get excited. He likes the idea of finally bringing the woman he loves together with his children. He has been feeling more connected to Angela and believes the time has come to take the relationship to the next level. He calls Angela, and she listens politely to his invitation, but says her children have soccer games, which she plans to attend. John asks what time the games start and end, hoping that Angela might be able to do both. Angela responds that her schedule is just too full and she can't join them. She tells John that she hopes they have a good day shopping and that she'll see him for their regular Thursday night date when her kids are with their father.

John, feeling a little defeated, says he understands and hopes her kids have great games. He hangs up and says to his daughter, "I guess it's just you and me." Janine jokingly tells her father that she's sure this woman named Angela doesn't really exist and must be an imaginary friend. John laughs but is aware that he feels sad and alone. He finally has a relationship with someone he truly cares for, only to spend most of his time without her. He quickly recovers by telling himself that Angela is a busy and devoted mother. He's sure that she cares for him and that as soon as soccer season is over, they'll spend more time together.

Two months pass and although he still sees Angela regularly, John finds himself missing her on weekends when she is with her kids. He decides to invite Angela and her kids over for a barbecue. He wants to meet Angela's children and wants Angela to meet his. John decides that he'll extend the invitation after dinner on

Thursday. Thursday night arrives. John tries to keep his invitation casual so that Angela will not know just how much he wants this. Instinctively he knows that Angela would not like feeling any pressure. He holds his breath in anticipation of her response.

Angela pauses. After a few moments she says, "That's really thoughtful of you, John, but I don't think we'll be able to make it. We already have plans and as you know, we decided a long time ago to keep our kids out of the mix. I'd rather we keep things that way. I like our time together alone, without having to deal with kids."

John looks down. He doesn't really know what to say. He tells Angela that he understands. He becomes quiet and rather aloof. He pays the bill and drives Angela home silently. When they arrive home, Angela says she's not feeling well and asks John if it would be okay if they called it a night and he went home. John, who hasn't said more than three words since they left the restaurant, replies, "That's fine, I understand." As John drives home, he finds himself feeling hopeless. His thoughts drift as he begins to digest reality as he now understands it.

Wow, You Weren't like This Before

John realizes that Angela does not want to create a blended family, at least not with him. At first John thought Angela was a protective mother, someone who wanted to make sure that he would be a positive male figure before bringing him into her children's lives. Now he's beginning to see things differently. Instead of seeing Angela as fun and easygoing, he is beginning to see her as wanting things her way and only her way. She gets to have fun, be nurtured, have sex, and enjoy their alone time without any hassles or responsibilities. She gets the benefits of having a nice and generous boyfriend while maintaining her freedom. It is becoming clear to John that Angela is not interested in meeting his needs. He is becoming increasingly hurt and disappointed, now sorting out who Angela really is and what he should do about it.

After John arrives home, he decides that Angela is a selfish, controlling person who is only interested in getting her needs met at the expense of others. He feels used and unloved. His hurt demeanor begins to shift and he starts to feel more angry and entitled. He decides that he needs to take a stronger stand for what he wants—a commitment to creating a blended family.

John misses the family time and experiences he had when married to his ex-wife. He wants this in his life. He wants this with Angela. He is sure that if he can only get her to agree to a family outing, she will see just how nice this could be. He's sure she'll come around and that her kids will like him. Surely once she sees this she'll be ready to move forward. Maybe she just needs a little more time.

Angela gets out of the car and goes inside her home, relieved to be alone. As she gets out of her clothes and into her nightgown, she finds herself feeling annoyed with John. Things had been going just fine. Their time together was pleasant. She likes having adult time without her children's involvement. She likes the time without any responsibilities. Having gone through a difficult divorce a few years back, she has no desire to start a new blended family. She is enjoying her freedom and doesn't want any pressures from anyone. The last thing Angela wants is to be accountable to another man. "Been there, done that," she thinks aloud.

As her annoyance begins to build a life of its own, Angela's feelings toward John change quickly. She cares about him but is beginning to see him as needy. He is calling her too many times during the week, asking her again and again to do things on the days she has her children. She is getting tired of having to say no, and even though John always says "I understand," Angela feels his disappointment. Tonight is a perfect example. When Angela turned down John's invitation for the barbecue, John looked down with a sad look on his face. He barely engaged in any conversation thereafter and when he did, he mumbled short, almost inaudible answers. His silence spoke volumes.

The man she once experienced as independent now seems more like a child. She is beginning to see that John's easygoing nature is not authentic. Instead, it's his way to manipulate her —if he is a good boy, then she will be a good mommy and do what he wants. Well, she has too many children of her own to raise and is certainly not interested in adding more. Why, when things were going so well, does John have to mess things up? Why couldn't he leave well enough alone and just be the fun, nurturing, take care of himself kind of guy she knew him to be these last six months? Somewhere in the middle of her silent ramblings, Angela feels her annoyance transmute into sadness and disappointment.

Let's stop and take a look at what we know:

1. John and Angela are learning new things about each other. They are now grappling with the reality of their different needs and wants.

2. As John's needs shift, so do his perceptions of Angela. The positive qualities he saw in Angela are now taking on a different tone. John is struggling with his disappointment.

3. Angela is reacting to John's attempts to change the rules of the game. She likes the lighthearted nature of their relationship. She doesn't want to deal with any conflict and thus rejects John's requests politely but consistently.

4. Angela sees John's vulnerabilities surface and is annoyed by the way he deals with trying to get his needs met and with his disappointment when they're not.

5. Both Angela and John are becoming real people. They are beginning to face how and why they react strongly to each other.

6. John and Angela are clearly moving out of phase one and into phase two.

While concerns are beginning to surface, neither Angela nor John is openly confronting the real issues. John retreats when he feels helpless and rejected. He is unable to effectively address his needs with Angela. On the other hand, Angela doesn't like direct confrontation. She politely declines John's invitations, but does so with a false sense of sincerity. She ignores John's pouting and goes on as if everything is fine. As long as John doesn't press the point, Angela will avoid any conflict and attempt to keep things light and fun. The tension is building. It will become more and more difficult for John and Angela to maintain the dance.

Although tensions are building, Angela and John have been with each other long enough to be sufficiently attached. Even in the face of disappointment and challenges, at this point neither one is walking away. This is in part due to several factors. First, their past six months together have, overall, been positive. Second, while the dopamine effect of excitement may be waning, oxytocin, the hormone of attachment, is alive and well. Third, while the illusion that they had found their perfect match is ending, there are still many qualities they like about each other. Lastly, ending relationships once an attachment has been made is not pain free. No one likes to feel rejected or abandoned. Dealing with loss is hard. Avoiding the work of letting go is as much a reason for couples to stay together as any other. These factors are what make it possible for Angela and John to stick things out and continue to explore the issues associated with phase two.

Angela and John will need to address several issues as they traverse through phase two. They need to

- Experience and understand the other for who the other really is

- Determine how much of that understanding is true, and how much of that is still their own projection and reactivity

- Discover aspects of themselves that contribute to the relationship dynamics

- Be able to test understanding and communicate their insights effectively

All these tasks are inherently difficult. Tackling them requires

- Insight and consciousness (to see what really is)
- Commitment and integrity (to the truth and taking responsibility for oneself)
- Communication (to be heard and understood; to hear and understand)

Let's see what happens next.

The Real Work Begins: Angela and John Confront Each Other

A couple of days pass and the feelings from the other night lessen. John regains his patience and decides not to push things with Angela. He believes that continuing to be a fun and easygoing playmate is the best strategy for getting closer to Angela. Angela's annoyance fades and after a demanding week at work, she longs to escape her usual responsibilities. The weekend arrives.

John calls her as usual on Friday afternoon and suggests they go out to dinner and a movie the following night.

At dinner they keep the conversation light. Neither one mentions the invitation for the barbecue or John's interest in beginning to establish family time with their children. Angela feels relieved as John appears to be his old self again. John feels less anxious and more hopeful. However, deep down John knows that in time his dissatisfaction and frustration will resurface. In the meantime, he continues to be good company for Angela, behaving in a way that makes her feel comfortable. The same dance continues for a few weeks longer until John receives an invitation from an old friend about their annual holiday get-together.

Every year John's friend throws a family and friend potluck gathering a week before Christmas. John always brings his kids, since they have known these family friends for many years. It's a tradition that John enjoyed with his ex-wife when they were married. After the divorce, John continued to join in the festivities, keeping the tradition alive for himself and his children. John's first impulse is to extend the invitation to Angela and her children but hesitates and then decides it is simply not worth the risk of further rejection.

He attends the holiday party with his children. During the party, he thinks about Angela. He looks around at all the other people there with their spouses. He longs to be one of them and feels lonely and empty. The feelings are familiar. He knows something needs to change. He cannot tolerate the way things are much longer. John plans his strategy while he drives his children back to their mother's home. He decides that this holiday will be different. He'll take a stand and re-quest that he and Angela spend some time together on Christmas with their respective children. After all, they have been together for almost nine months. Certainly this has earned him the right to make some demands that his needs be met. His strength and fortitude grow as he gathers his courage to make this final invitation.

It is now two days before Christmas. John and Angela are sitting down, enjoying a glass of wine before deciding where to go for dinner. Angela's children are with their father. John finally gets his nerve. He tells Angela that he would really like to spend some time with her on Christmas. Maybe, he tells her, they can use the holiday as an opportunity for the families to come together. He tells her he thinks it's time.

But Angela politely tells him that she and her children already have plans. She says, "I don't think I want to put that kind of pressure on anyone given that it's a holiday. I mean really, my kids and I have our own traditions. I'm sure you and your children have yours. I think it's best for everyone that we each keep our own."

John is flabbergasted. He can't fathom what he is hearing. His frustration returns with a fury. He feels like the person in front of him is a complete stranger. He thought he knew Angela, but now he's not sure of anything.

Angela is beside herself. She cannot believe that John is at it again and on a holiday no less. Her patience is exhausted. She feels disgusted by his neediness and inability to let things be. She may not know much, but at least she knows this—no one is going to enter her sacred family circle. Not John, not anyone.

What John and Angela Don't Know

What John doesn't know is that Angela came from a family where there were intense fights between her father and just about everyone else. Her father was an alcoholic who had angry outbursts that both frightened and traumatized Angela. She coped by keeping the peace and never creating a stir. She developed a knack at pretending everything was okay amid the chaos. She kept a smile on her face and went about her business as if nothing wrong was going on. The shouting matches, pushing, and ongoing drama that played out in her family life resulted in a little girl stuffing her feelings and her needs inside. Angela saw her mother take a lot of abuse but stay in the marriage regardless. She decided long ago that her mother was too weak and needy to leave. Angela's mother had no college degree and little work experience. Angela dismissed her mother's own past and circumstances and was determined to make her own life different. She learned to associate neediness and dependence on others with trauma and pain. Angela wanted nothing to do with any of it. She grew up denying her own needs and had little tolerance for neediness in others. Deep down, she was still a hurt, angry little girl with plenty of unmet needs.

Angela married young and moved away with her husband in part because it was the easiest way to leave her alcoholic family. They had children fairly young, but in spite of this, Angela managed to go back to school and get her nursing degree. Angela's ex-husband was a nondrinker, but very controlling. His constant jealousy and need to control everything finally drove Angela to divorce. She was strong enough to know she could make it on her own and was no longer willing to live with someone so controlling. She may have made that mistake once but was determined to never let anyone control her or her life again. She refuses to become her mother.

What Angela doesn't know about John is that he came from quite a different family. From the outside, John's parents looked like the perfect mother and father living the perfect family life. John's father, a judge, was well respected in the community and held himself and others to a very high standard of achievement. His mother was extremely independent and successful. She worked many hours in a high paying, highly demanding sales position for a pharmaceutical company. Both his parents worked long and hard, providing all the material comforts and educational opportunities a child could want. However, what John desperately wanted most—time and attention—he didn't get. Only a slew of nannies and other caregivers provided him with this.

John was an only child and felt very alone while growing up. He worked hard to be a good son and student. It was the way he learned to get his parents' approval, love, and attention. When this strategy failed, John retreated into himself. At times, he would silently mope around the house in hopes that his parents would notice his discontent and respond accordingly. Sometimes this worked, sometimes not. John's parents were very involved with their professional and social lives. As long as John was doing well in school, sports, and other extracurricular activities, they were confident that all was well. John secretly fantasized that one day he would have a family of his own and finally get his needs for love and family belonging met.

John got married a few years out of college after establishing himself in his career as an engineer. He and his wife had three children. He thought everything was fine in their marriage and enjoyed all the rewards that family life had to offer. What he didn't know was that his wife was bored, unfulfilled, and depressed. She eventually had an affair and left John for another man. John was devastated. It took him many years to give up on his fantasy that he could somehow get his family back together. Since his divorce, he remained a devoted father, spending a lot of time doing things with his kids. He chose to put his romantic life on hold, only dating casually and occasionally. When he didn't have his kids, he kept to himself, often feeling abandoned and lonely. When John met Angela his hope revived. He was sure that this was the woman with whom he could create a new family and a sense of security and well-being that had been lacking in his life.

Back to their story:

John responds by shaking his head in utter disbelief, now almost pleading with her to do just this one thing for him. "How can you be so selfish and heartless? It's Christmas for God's sake! Don't my needs count for anything here or is it only the Angela Show?"

John's words startle Angela. She's never heard him push back like this. His confrontation opens a door that until now has been kept shut. Pandora's box has been opened and there is no turning back. Angela can no longer contain her irritation. "Selfish and heartless? You have got to be kidding. I've been nothing but polite, pleasant, and good-natured. Why can't you understand my desire to spend Christmas with my children and not with you and your children. You are the neediest, most pathetic man I've ever met. I'm not here to make your world complete. I'm not here to make you feel less pathetic."

With that John turns around and heads out the door. He cannot take any more rejection and humiliation. As he walks out he says, "I may be needy, but what I want isn't unreasonable. Maybe you should take a look at why you're so reluctant to let me and my children into your life. Maybe you should look at yourself for a change."

John goes to his car but cannot get himself to start it. He feels as though his world is crashing down around him, that his hopes of having a loving family are destroyed. Although he loves Angela, he feels helpless and hopeless about his future with her. He finally starts the car. As he drives, he keeps thinking about the confrontation. "Maybe I shouldn't have asked. I knew what her answer would be anyway. Why are my needs on the bottom of everyone's priority list? Why am I destined to be alone and ignored?"

By the time he arrives home, John is completely depressed. He pours himself a drink, sits down on the couch, and soon falls asleep.

Angela is now in a full-blown rage. How dare he point his finger at her! Her request to keep her Christmas with her children private is not unreasonable; his request is. What a jerk! She continues to yell at John in her head, repeating how he is really a screwed-up guy and needs therapy. She keeps telling herself that she really needs to cut this guy loose and move on. She deserves a more together, independent man who doesn't need constant reassurance. Angela is so upset that she decides to call her best friend Christine and tell her what happened. Surely Christine will concur that this guy is a loser and needs to go. Surely Christine would agree that Angela had done nothing wrong and that John is the unreasonable one. Yes, she'll call Christine.

Angela tells Christine what has happened down to the very last detail and words exchanged. Christine listens attentively. Christine has sympathy for Angela, expressing how sorry she is that things have gone downhill in the relationship. Then Christine does what all good friends do—she lets Angela know how much she understands her plight. Christine begins by saying, "You know Angela, I completely understand why you want to keep John and his kids at a distance. With what you went through with your family and ex-husband any sane woman would do the same. I don't know how you survived all that you did. You certainly don't need another man in your life to control you and your children. And you certainly don't need any more drama. John just doesn't know what I know. He doesn't know how selfless you've been all your life. He doesn't know how much you had to sacrifice just to keep things from erupting. John takes all this personally. He doesn't understand that it will take you a very long time before you'll trust another man with your heart and soul. He doesn't get that all this has absolutely nothing to do with him."

Angela listens silently. As Christine talks, Angela feels her anger soften. Her annoyance disappears. Her righteousness turns into humility. She is surprised by the change in her feelings. After Christine stops talking,

Angela sits in silence for a minute and then finally says sadly, "You're right. John doesn't understand any of this."

The conversation continues for a few more minutes and then Angela gets off the phone. She begins to ask herself some questions. What did John really do that was so wrong? Why did she react so strongly? Why was this issue so important to her? Was she really a control freak? Why was she so unwilling to compromise? Why did she feel like crying when only moments ago she felt so indignant and angry? Angela searches for answers. She looks to her past and she looks at her fears. She begins to understand why she reacted the way she did. And as she understands herself more, she tries to understand where John may be coming from as well.

Angela is surprised to discover that she and John have more in common than she thought. "All John wanted was to feel included in my life and to include me in his," thought Angela. "Having a close and loving family was important to him." That was something Angela could understand. She had longed to feel loved and cared for growing up. Instead, she remembers how scared she felt most of the time. She remembers how it became safer to simply deny all her needs rather than feel the pain when they were unmet. Angela was beginning to consider that John may have had his own version of the same growing up.

She begins to feel a kinship with John. Compassion replaces judgment. At least John can ask for his needs; she hadn't given herself permission to have those kinds of needs for a very long time. It just feels too risky. It feels like her life would be at stake. Maybe John isn't as pathetic as she thought. Maybe he was just trying to get his needs met, albeit in an annoying manner. Angela smiles as she thinks about how childlike John gets when he feels rejected. She smiles even more and laughs out loud when she realizes how unreasonably she behaved. Maybe Christine was right. Maybe she needs to be in control. Maybe she isn't ready to let anyone into her world.

Angela's thoughts continue to flow through her mind. She gains more and more clarity. She understands what buttons got triggered. Angela realizes that there is still a lot of pain underneath the surface. She gets just how scared she is to trust anyone. She understands that John is not the bad guy here. No one is. And despite all these incredibly powerful insights, Angela still can't pick up the phone and invite John and his kids over for Christmas. She's not ready to include John and his kids into her sacred family circle. She's sure about this, but less sure what she wants to do next. Should she call him or wait for him to call her? What will she say?

John awakens from his deep sleep on the couch unsettled. The memory of his argument with Angela drifts back into his mind. He remembers his parting words to Angela, "Maybe you should look at yourself for a change." He feels guilty. He is so conditioned to be the nice, well-behaved boy that even an honest confrontation makes him feel that he was too harsh. To combat this feeling, John decides to heed his own advice. Why is this issue so important to him? Why does he always feel like his needs don't matter? Why does he feel so alone?

John reflects back on all the times he saw his parents put their needs before his. He always felt alone and left out. He realizes that Angela's stand on keeping him at a distance triggered those feelings. He remembers moping around the house as a boy, hoping that his parents would notice his unhappiness. He chuckles to himself as he realizes he still behaves in the same manner. John shakes his head, admitting that he probably does look pretty needy and pathetic. He wonders why he's always attracted to women who put their needs before his. What's that all about? He always feels like he's left with the short stick.

John continues to access his memories. He creates his laundry list of rejections. His parents were busy with their work and friends, his wife had an affair and destroyed their family, and now Angela refuses to let him into her life. Why was he always left out? One thing is clear. He always feels like a victim. Hmm. This conclusion doesn't sit well with John. No wonder Angela doesn't respect him. No wonder she gets annoyed. John begins to feel disgusted with himself. He definitely needs to make a change. Maybe he needs to figure out a way to be less needy. Maybe he needs to figure out a way to ask for what he wants with power. Maybe he needs to learn to handle disappointment with more maturity. Maybe he needs to learn how to cut his losses if someone is simply not a good match. While John isn't sure he has all the answers just yet, he knows he at least has the right questions. Immediately he feels less like a victim. He is committed to getting his needs met more powerfully and accepting with more grace when he does not.

John thinks about Angela. What is she so afraid of? Why can't she let him in? Maybe instead of quickly concluding that Angela was simply selfish and cruel, he should ask more questions. Maybe there is something he doesn't know. Angela might have reasons for not wanting to blend their families that made sense to her. Just because she hadn't offered up any real explanations other than that she liked things the way they were didn't mean those reasons didn't exist. John admits that he was so busy reacting to Angela's rejection with his usual passivity that he never inquired more into how Angela felt and why. Really, how many "I understands" can one man express? He laughs aloud as he considers that maybe he is the selfish one, not Angela.

John decides to let things cool down for a few days. He'll call Angela to wish her a merry Christmas and suggest that they meet later that week and talk. He'll let her know that he has realized some things about himself that he would like to share with her. He's sure that if they can have an open and honest conversation, they'll be able to correct any misunderstandings and move forward from there. For the first time in a long time, John feels hopeful about his relationship with Angela. In fact, he feels remarkably better about everything. John makes himself a sandwich and settles in for an evening of late-night television.

Let's stop and take a look at what we know:

1. Angela's and John's reactions to each other intensify. They can no longer sustain the façade of solely revealing their polite personas. They begin to reveal their true selves—issues, warts, and all.

2. Their reactions stem from a combination of their own projections onto the other and experiencing more of the real Angela and John.

3. Angela and John have to deal with their disappointments. The fantasy phase has ended. Angela and John are neither perfect nor perfect matches after all. The relationship is going to require something from both of them if it's going to grow and flourish.

4. Angela and John process their reactivity in their own ways. Initially, Angela talks to a friend; John has a drink and takes a nap.

Once their reactivity is neutralized, they are both able to reflect, test reality, and see things differently.

5. Several insights and inquiries are made. These include

  i. understanding what button got pushed and why;

  ii. separating out what actually occurred from what they made it mean;

  iii. recognizing when they lost their power and how to get it back;

  iv. sorting out what they knew about the other and what they did not;

  v. identifying their own projections;

  vi. understanding their needs, how important are those needs, and how to get them met;

  vii. bringing their fears to a conscious level and deciding what to do with them if anything.

Angela and John now need to decide what to do next. They have discovered several things about themselves. They have discovered different things about the other. They understand how much they still don't know. There are several options from which to choose. They can share their insights. They can ask questions to learn and understand the other. Angela and John can make requests. They can negotiate getting their needs met. They can do nothing and walk away. Angela and John can do one, some, or all of the above.

Phase two is really about self-discovery. Angela and John are clearly engaged in the developmental tasks at hand. Regardless of what they decide to do next, they have already been successful.

Angela and John: What Happened Next?

Over the next several days, Angela and John continue to reflect on what happened and what there is to learn. They also continue to consider how they want to proceed. John feels confident that he can resolve the misunderstanding with Angela. He wants to share his thoughts on what happened and ask Angela to share more of her concerns about deepening their relationship.

Angela feels clearer about what got triggered. She's comfortable taking full responsibility for her reactions, rather than blaming John for having his needs. Angela is also clear that she is not ready to take any emotional risks just yet. There is a lot of healing that still needs to occur. She is sure she is not willing to give up control and be vulnerable the way John wants her to be. Angela decides that she's better off putting her energy into getting some counseling rather than working through these issues in a serious relationship. She realizes that she simply isn't ready yet for what John wants and it would be unfair to John for her to pretend otherwise.

John calls Angela the day after Christmas. They are both a little timid at first on the phone, feeling their respective vulnerabilities. They start by inquiring how each other's Christmas had been. After a few minutes of polite small talk, John breaks the tension. "Angela, I've been thinking about what happened. I'm really sorry I called you selfish. I overreacted because when I was growing up, I felt alone most of the time. My parents were very involved with their work and I never felt like I had a 'real' family. I care about you a lot and really want to create that 'family' with you. I understand that you feel differently and I wish I had reacted with more maturity than I did. I guess that little boy still lives inside me. I don't believe that you're selfish. I know better. I would, though, like to understand more why you're hesitant to move forward with our relationship. I really think we can resolve your concerns."

Angela takes a deep breath. "No apologies necessary. We both overreacted. But here's the thing. I've also been thinking a lot about what happened. I've come to realize that regardless of the reasons, I'm just not ready to make that kind of commitment to anyone. I have some things to work out for myself and I don't think it's fair to you to keep you from finding someone who is. I'm not sure when, if at all, I'll be ready and I don't want to continue to disappoint you. I really can't handle the pressure and guilt."

"Can you tell me your reasons? I'd really like to know."

"I don't want to go into it with you. I really just want to let you know that I care about you and have enjoyed our time together. I truly hope that you find someone that feels the same way that you do. I want you to be happy."

"So that's it? You don't want to talk about this and see if we can find a compromise that works for both of us?"

"No, I don't. I think it's best if we just let things be and end on a positive note."

"Okay. I guess there's nothing else I can do. Can I at least call you in a couple of months and see how you are?"

"That would be fine, John. I'm really sorry. I hope you have a good New Year."

They say good-bye and hang up the phone. John is caught off guard by Angela's seemingly abrupt decision. He was sure that they could talk about what had happened and find a way to get past it. His emotions run through anger, sadness, confusion, and disappointment. He sits down, staring into space, trying to digest what just happened. He finds himself fighting the reality. When his rational mind takes hold, he knows he has no choice but to accept Angela's decision. Just as John begins to accept what is, a spark of hope flies into his heart. He remembered that they agreed he would call her in a couple of months and see if anything's changed. At least that's how he remembers things. Maybe she'll miss him and want him back. Maybe she'll have worked through some of her issues.

Having restored some hope, John keeps his grief at bay. John knows that if he allows himself to be resigned to Angela's decision, he runs the risk of falling into a deep depression. While John knows he will miss Angela, he finds solace in holding on to the hope of a happy ending for yet another two months.

Angela, however, feels relieved. Although she knows she will miss the fun, carefree time she spent with John, she will not miss the recent pressure to make the relationship be something more. She is not ready for that and does not want to share any of her authentic self with him. She starts preparing dinner for her kids, thankful to have her space and sense of control back. She decides that after the New Year, she will obtain counseling. She knows that she has past trauma that requires professional help. While she is not interested in sharing any of this with John, she is committed to her own growth and well-being. A good therapist is what's called for, not a needy boyfriend. She hopes that John doesn't contact her again. Hopefully, he will have moved on in a couple months' time and not reach out. Angela knows she needs to figure some things out before getting into another relationship. She is definitely not in any hurry to start dating someone else.

The End of Phase Two

When you and the person you're with begin to reveal your true selves and take responsibility for your reactions, interpretations, and choices, there is an incredible opportunity for self-discovery. This is the time to confront yourself by taking a good look in the mirror. In the context of relationships, the mirror is your significant other. How you see her, how you react to her and how she reacts to you is your window into yourself. When you can inquire and reflect honestly on your and your significant other's thoughts, feelings, and actions, the opportunities for growth expand. In doing so, you are able to understand, accept, and love yourself and your significant other for who each of you truly is.

This does not necessarily mean that the relationship will continue. It does not mean that the relationship should continue. Regardless of the outcome, the gifts that are available in discovering yourself through the eyes of another are worth having come this far. It is through self-discovery that healing and transformation occurs. By taking on the developmental tasks that phase two offers, genuine love of self and others becomes possible.

In the case of Angela and John, their relationship ended. However, all was not lost. They both discovered valuable things about themselves. John realized how much he projected his childhood experiences onto his adult relationships. He also became aware that he still managed his needs and emotions in the same passive way he did as a child. He understood that his assumptions and conclusions may not be accurate. In essence, John's unconscious way of relating to Angela became conscious. He was able to separate out what he knew from what he didn't. In addition, John decided he was committed to doing things differently. He knew he needed to communicate and manage his needs more effectively. Through the eyes of Angela, John discovered things about himself that would enable him to make more conscious, powerful choices in his future relationships.

Angela, on the other hand, was able to acknowledge her deepest fears. She became aware of how she managed her fears by keeping others at a distance. She learned how she keeps control, even when she thinks she is just keeping the peace. Her willingness to take ownership of her reactions to John enabled her to stop projecting. In doing so, she opened up the possibility that relationships could be different from those in her past. In addition, Angela was able to be honest with herself about where she stood in terms of her readiness for change. She owned her own resistances. She knew she had wounds that required more time to heal. She honored and identified how best to take care of herself and her needs. And although she chose not to share any intimate information with John, she ended the relationship in an honest and powerful way.

John wanted to create a more authentic and intimate relationship. He wanted to move on to phase three. Angela wanted to take the time to heal past wounds by herself. Neither Angela's nor John's choice was wrong. Each made a powerful choice for themselves. They honored themselves, thereby successfully completing phase two.

In summary, phase two is really about

- Beginning to distinguish who your significant other really is from who you still want or fear them to be

- Learning to deal with disappointment, conflict, and loss more effectively

- Understanding your needs and wants; understanding your significant other's needs and wants

- Identifying your own unresolved issues and how they get triggered within the relationship

- Taking full responsibility for your reactions and assumptions

- Relating to yourself and your significant other with compassion and understanding

- Making powerful choices in how to best take care of yourself and your needs even if that means walking away from the relationship

- Creating a more meaningful bond and attachment that goes beyond your projections and the *dopamine-oxytocin effect*

While many couples will naturally move into phase three, other couples may choose to stay in phase two or fluctuate between phase one and phase two indefinitely. This occurs when one or both people are able to self-reflect but are unable or unwilling to authentically share and communicate with each other what they have discovered about themselves. Couples can stay in phase two for a lifetime. Their communication is more concrete and superficial in nature, focusing only on things that are safe to talk about. Personal defenses are still strongly in place. They may not be able to fully tolerate the pain that comes from connecting with past trauma. And while they may have a deeper understanding of themselves, they are still unable to be truly vulnerable with their partner. They may appear close from the outside looking in, but their relationship lacks any true authenticity and intimacy. There tends to still be blame and power struggles over who's right and who's wrong as well as a need to look good to themselves and others.

Relationships typically end when one person no longer accepts staying stuck in phases one and two. The need to create and experience deep intimacy and love is too strong. When that person's partner is not willing or able to move on to the work of phase three, the person who doesn't want to stay stuck will need to either accept things as they are or leave the relationship. If he cannot accept his partner's choice and doesn't leave, he runs the risk of becoming depressed, ill, or addicted in some fashion.

Relationships move into phase three when both parties are able and ready to accept each other for who they truly are and communicate authentically. This is when two people are in their full power and the experience of love is transformative.

Let's explore phase three through Kevin and Sophie.

Phase Three: Personal Transformation

A Marriage Tested: The Story of Kevin and Sophie

Kevin and Sophie have been married for eight years. They have one son who is five years old. Up until now, Kevin and Sophie have been functioning fairly successfully, moving in and out of phases one and two. They have been busy adjusting to each other and settling into living as husband and wife and raising their young son. Something is about to happen that will rock their relatively peaceful world and test their marriage. It will be a make or break time that will force them to do the real work of phase two, move into phase three, or risk pending disaster.

Before we hear their story, let's get to know Kevin and Sophie a bit more.

Kevin is a 38-year-old account executive for an electronics firm. He prides himself on being very professional and prefers order and control to disarray and uncertainty. Kevin holds himself to high standards and is silently self-deprecating when he believes he hasn't met them. In turn, Kevin can judge others harshly when they do not conform to his standards for competency and order. He likes his personal and professional life to be well structured and planned out, avoids spontaneity whenever possible, and can be intolerant to others who are different from him.

Sophie is a 33-year-old beautician who works part-time for a local salon and spends the rest of her time tending to her family and home. She works hard to please others, making sure their needs get met, often at the expense of her own. She is not a complainer, is very empathic, and enjoys making people happy. She lacks confidence and has low self-worth. She compensates for this self-image by doing what she can to support her husband's success. She spends a lot of time and energy anticipating the needs and issues of friends and family and responding to them. She takes pride in her ability to help people feel good about themselves. Unlike her husband, she is very spontaneous. She has to be in order to react quickly to others' anxieties and adjust her behavior in order to contain any unexpressed tension.

As you can guess, Kevin and Sophie have been a perfect match, at least until now.

Kevin and Sophie met ten years ago at a mutual friend's party. They hit it off and had a positive projective fantasy of each other. While they were dating, they had little conflict. Kevin was very reliable, predictable, and responsible. Sophie went out of her way to please Kevin and make sure his world was comfortable. If there was a conflict in needs, wants, or interests, Sophie unconsciously acquiesced to Kevin and found a way to justify doing things his way as opposed to hers. She learned quickly that Kevin needed an orderly environment. She always made sure the house was clean and orderly before Kevin arrived home so that she did not have to feel his disapproval and tension. This precedent was established very early on—Sophie would accommodate her behavior in order to prevent any meltdowns from Kevin. Kevin would find subtle and sometimes not so subtle ways to let Sophie know when he needed a greater sense of control. Sophie would respond accordingly, as much to avoid her own anxieties about her life and her future as to take care of Kevin's need to avoid his anxieties and fears.

In the beginning, this unconscious arrangement worked. Although the underlying pressure increased somewhat after they got married, the dance that they had created was intricate enough to effectively avert any mounting tension and restore equilibrium to the relationship. After the birth of their son, Sophie's anxieties grew as she struggled with how to be a good mother. She was overwhelmed with a newborn but said nothing to Kevin. She just worked harder to be a good wife and mother, complained little to none, and tried to keep Kevin's life structured and happy. As a result, the family enjoyed their time together and spent many happy times doing fun activities. Kevin was a good father, very attentive to his son and loyal to his wife, and felt that life was pretty good. Work was stressful and demanding at times, but overall he liked the company he worked for and planned on having a good career there for many years to come.

Kevin and Sophie appeared to be the all-American family and, for the most part, they had found a way to work through tensions. Their approach was not very sophisticated or insightful, but it worked partly because both Kevin and Sophie weren't that interested in exploring their inner worlds. They liked the simple and comfortable life they had created together and neither wanted to rock the boat. Up until now, they had been able to maintain that life and the illusion of control.

However, things are about to change very quickly.

The Illusion of Control Is Shattered

It's the Friday before spring break. Kevin and Sophie have planned a vacation with their son. They're going to fly to Florida and enjoy the magic of Disney World and other attractions. They booked the trip months before, believing that their son was now old enough to enjoy the attractions. They want to create fun family memories. Kevin shows up early to work so he can tie up loose ends and leave business worries behind for the following week. Shortly after he arrives, his boss phones Kevin and asks him to come into his office. Kevin is surprised to see his boss there that early but figures his boss also wants to get some things done before the holiday weekend. Kevin thinks nothing of it as he hangs up the phone and walks over to his boss's office.

Kevin sits down. His boss looks uncomfortable and serious. It's then that Kevin notices the director of human resources is also present. Kevin suddenly feels anxious. His boss tells him in a direct and matter-of-fact way that the company lost their two major accounts earlier that week, both of which were Kevin's. They had no choice but to respond quickly to the sudden and significant loss in revenue. After several executive meetings, a decision was made to downsize immediately. Unfortunately, Kevin's position needs to be cut as the majority of his accounts are no longer with the company. Kevin's boss hands him a severance check, apologizes for the suddenness of the action, and reassures him that this is in no way a reflection of his abilities. He goes on to explain that given Kevin's level of seniority and the fact that these two accounts were his, they have no choice but to let him go. Kevin's boss asks that he empty out his desk and, when he is ready, he will be escorted out of the building. He reassures Kevin that this is simply protocol. Kevin is blindsided. He leaves the office in shock and disbelief and heads back down the hall to his office, where he finds some empty boxes waiting for him.

Kevin packs up his personal belongings in a trance and is escorted by security to his car. When he gets into his car, he opens the envelope that holds his severance check and finds it's for three months of salary. Three months. Kevin has been with the company for six years. While he is responsible with his finances, his and Sophie's savings are very slim, as they have put all their money into the house they bought four years ago. Their mortgage is fairly high. Kevin knows the severance money will not last long. Unemployment benefits, along with his wife's small part-time income, will not even come close to covering their expenses. Kevin's shock and disbelief slowly turns into panic.

Kevin arrives home just as his wife returns from having dropped off their son at school. She does not have any work scheduled because she planned on getting things organized for their trip to Florida the next day. When Kevin gets out of the car, she stands in the driveway, looking at him with confusion. "What are you doing home so soon? Is everything all right?" Kevin tells her he has just been laid off. He picks up his box of files from his car and proceeds to the front door. "What?" says Sophie as if she did not hear him correctly. As Kevin walks through the front door with his back to his wife he repeats that he has been laid off. He goes upstairs to their bedroom, closes the door, and sits down on the bed.

Sophie lets the words sink in until she is sure she has heard him accurately. Panic fills her body. A million thoughts go through her mind. What will they do? What about their vacation to Florida? Will she need to disappoint her son and tell him they won't be going after all? What's going to happen to their home, their life? What is Kevin going to do? She immediately fears the worst. They will lose their home. Times are really tough, and jobs are almost impossible to find. Also, Kevin will not handle this setback well. What will happen to her and her son? She only has a handful of customers at the salon and doesn't see how she will be able to increase her client base while still being there for her son and husband. Sophie doesn't know what to do. She goes inside the house and heads for the bedroom door.

Sophie wants desperately to reassure and help her husband. After all, it's her job to keep things in control so that her husband can feel comfortable. She opens the door and starts to tell Kevin that she knows he must be very upset but that she's sure everything will be just fine. She goes to put her arms around him to comfort him, to let him know that she is there for him and will do anything he needs to help him get through this. As she reaches out to hug him, Kevin pulls away and snaps, "I really don't need this right now. I need you to go away and let me figure things out. You're no help to me whatsoever, so please just leave me alone."

Sophie is stunned. All she was doing was trying to comfort and reassure him. All she wanted was to be helpful and supportive, and what did she get in return? Anger and rejection. Sophie leaves the room. She goes downstairs and sits at the kitchen table, staring at the family photos and art projects displayed on the refrigerator door. She starts to cry. She feels so hurt and helpless, like her existence in this marriage doesn't matter. She feels like an outsider to a world her husband lives in without her, one in which she is not welcomed. She has never felt so alone in the eight years that she and her husband have lived together. In this moment, she feels like their marriage is a farce and their world is falling apart.

Kevin knows he has hurt his wife's feelings but can't get up and apologize for his outburst. He's in too much pain. He doesn't know how he'll manage to take care of his family financially and is questioning his abilities as a man. He feels like a complete failure—as a man, a husband, a father, and a professional. Certainly he must have screwed up in order to have lost two major accounts for his company. How could he not have seen this coming? Why didn't his account reps let him know about this directly? Clearly the company didn't see any value in keeping him on and blamed him for its troubles. He questions every decision, every action, every move he has made in the last six months while managing these accounts. He feels utterly useless, powerless, and worthless. He isn't sure how he will recover from this blow but knows he will have to suck it up and find a way to secure another job.

Everything Kevin thought was true about himself and his life feels like a lie. He is powerless, and if he is powerless to take care of business, his wife is certainly in no position to make a difference. There isn't a word, hug, or gesture that can fix things. Her nice dinners and comfortable home furnishings do not provide any comfort or usefulness in this crisis. Right now he needs a game plan. He needs to keep it together; if he doesn't, he isn't sure what he will do. Kevin no longer trusts his instincts. He no longer trusts himself.

A few hours pass. Kevin comes downstairs and finds Sophie still sitting in the kitchen staring out the window. Kevin tells her to cancel their trip. They simply can't afford to go. He tells her that he's going out and doesn't know when he'll be back so she should plan on having dinner without him. The only response Sophie can muster is an "okay." With that, Kevin is out the door.

During the following few weeks, Kevin and Sophie live in a kind of cold war. Whenever Sophie tries to emotionally connect with Kevin and offer support or reassurance, she's met with a cold, quick response that basically reiterates, "Just leave me alone; I will figure this out on my own." Sophie is becoming more and more upset. She feels left out and rejected, as if she is incapable of contributing anything to improve their situation. It's as if her ideas and proposals for any solutions are met with a mocking, patronizing response. She realizes that her husband really doesn't have much respect for her and concludes that there really has been no partnership at all in their marriage. Clearly, the only thing that she's good for is keeping a clean orderly home, caring for their son, and making regularly scheduled meals. She feels her usefulness to her husband is superficial and condescending.

Her hurt begins to turn into anger and resentment. She's tired of being shut out and discounted. Her compassion for her husband and what has happened is quickly being replaced with apathy. Maybe his boss had good reasons to let him go; maybe he wasn't the genius at work that he thought he was. Sophie begins to blame her husband for their current crisis. The crevasse that is forming between them is growing deeper by the day. Sophie continues to care for their son, clean house, and prepare meals as usual. She tells her salon manager that she would appreciate any new clients the manager can send her way, explaining that her husband has been laid off from work. In the meantime, Sophie decides to create flyers advertising her services and distributes them around town. She is no longer interested in waiting for her husband's approval. She decides she needs to take things into her own hands and make some decisions for herself. As time goes on and Sophie continues to take action, she feels her confidence grow.

Kevin, on the other hand, is busy updating his resume, posting it online, and making calls to everyone he knows that might have a lead for a job. He keeps as busy as he can, but in the back of his mind that gnawing feeling of failure persists. His confidence is shattered, and deep down he's scared that the worst is still ahead of him. He feels like his life is completely out of his control. The only thing he knows is that he has to get out of bed and do something every day to look for work. If he doesn't, he's sure his life will fall to pieces. He knows he is pushing his wife away, and secretly knows why, but he can't stop himself. His sanity and their future are on the line. He just needs to stay disengaged. There is too much at risk for him if he doesn't.

The Tension Breaks: Kevin and Sophie Face the Truth

Week four passes and the tension in the house is mounting. Kevin detaches more and more from Sophie and their son. Sophie grows more and more angry and resentful, secretly taking matters into her own hands without conferring with Kevin. They are now living separate lives. They speak only when they need to and usually around issues related to their son. The crisis continues to build and their marriage suffers.

One day Kevin is out getting a cup of coffee and searching the Internet on his laptop for job openings. He looks up at the bulletin board on the coffeehouse wall where people put personal ads for neighborhood services, items for sale, lost dogs, and so on. One ad catches his eye. He recognizes his wife's name on the advertisement for hair cutting services. The flyer advertises salon services provided in the comfort of the customer's home, hours and days flexible, references available upon request. Kevin is stunned. He takes the advertisement down, finishes his cup of coffee, closes his laptop, and heads home. The silence will finally be broken.

Kevin feels his anger surge, although on some level he's unclear as to why discovering the advertisement makes him so angry. He has no time to reflect, nor does he want to. He just wants to rage, and this seems like the perfect opportunity. At home he finds Sophie folding the laundry. His son is still at school. He immediately shoves the advertisement in her face and shouts, "What the hell is this? Are you planning on starting your own business without telling me? Why are you sneaking around? What kind of business is this? Who are you to be doing anything without my permission? Who do you think you are? Rachael Ray?" Kevin's rant lasts for five solid minutes.

Sophie stands there listening to someone who feels like a total stranger. Kevin has never spoken to her like this in all the time she's known him. Although she instinctively has known that underneath Kevin's controlled calm exterior lies anger, she has successfully kept it at bay all these years. Sophie has never imagined he could say the things he is saying to her now.

After he spews his final assaults, Sophie feels fear racing through her body. The adrenaline is palpable. Suddenly, her fear turns into anger, anger that has been building for the past few weeks, maybe for the past eight years. Regardless, the surge comes up through her body and into her throat. She tries to fight back the rush, but it's no use. A new sense of power and resolve emerges. Standing her ground, Sophie replies, "Who the hell do you think you are? You have said probably all of ten words to me since you lost your job, you won't let me know what you're doing or feeling, and you don't care how I'm doing or feeling. You have made me feel like I was a useless child that should be pushed aside so that you could figure things out on your own. I have been rejected, ignored, and insulted. You have treated me as if I have nothing to contribute, nothing to say in the matter, as if I simply do not count, as if I should continue to do the dishes and fold the laundry because that's all I'm good for. How insulting! Who do you think you are? Donald Trump? I did what I had to do, something to save this family from financial ruin. You sure aren't taking care of business so someone has to."

The assaults continue back and forth for the next few minutes until they have emptied out the tension that has been building for days, weeks, maybe years, possibly a lifetime. After the dust settles, Sophie tells Kevin she's going to pick up their son from school and leaves. Kevin feels shaken. Sophie is heartbroken. Never in a million years could either of them have believed they could treat each other that way. They feel their world crumbling. The rules of the game have changed. The game has changed. And neither one knows what to do about it.

Let's stop and take a look at what we know:

1. Sophie and Kevin have spent their marriage vacillating between phase one and phase two.

2. On the one hand, they have some awareness of how they project and protect each other from taking real responsibility for themselves; on the other hand, they do the dance fairly unconsciously.

3. They relate to each other as real people as opposed to solely objects, but lack sufficient self-awareness in order to understand how they project their hidden needs onto each other.

4. The dance of bouncing somewhere between phase one and phase two has worked well as long as there were no real crises that challenged their usual defense mechanisms.

5. Once a serious crisis occurred that could not be contained in their usual manner, their relationship quickly disintegrated. This is quite common in relationships that do not have a solid foundation laid in phase two.

6. Kevin and Sophie are now challenged with understanding themselves and each other more profoundly. Deep unresolved issues are surfacing. There is now an opening for transforming themselves and their relationship.

Relationships move into phase three most commonly when a crisis occurs. It is less common, though quite possible, for a couple to move into phase three without a crisis when both parties are committed to and proactively work on their personal growth and the development of intimacy in their relationship.

Crisis Becomes the Gateway to Intimacy and Phase Three

First Step: Self-Responsibility

Kevin breaks down and cries. He can't remember the last time he cried. Once his anger settles, Kevin realizes the emotion he feels is fear. He realizes that he is so afraid of so many things. He knows that his fear is not only running his life now but has probably been unconsciously running his life for years. All the fears he has worked so hard to bury come seeping in. He knows that the only way through his fears will be to confess them to the one person he loves and trusts the most, Sophie. He knows he will have to risk humiliation and rejection. He knows his marriage is at stake. He knows this is the only way to salvage his life.

Sophie cannot believe what has transpired only moments ago. She knows that this crisis is a turning point. She and Kevin will be able to work through this and be stronger because of it, or their relationship will fall apart. While she feels hurt and disappointed by the way Kevin spoke to her, she also feels relieved. It's as if she and Kevin have spent a lifetime holding back. What they have been holding on to, she is less sure of. But although she feels a little guilty for laying into Kevin, she feels freer than ever before. What has she been so afraid of all these years? Why was her life dedicated to keeping Kevin emotionally and physically comfortable at the expense of her own self-worth? When did she agree to lose herself and make her family more important?

Sophie knows that she and Kevin need time to deal with things in a more real and authentic manner. She realizes that their communication and relationship up until now have been fairly superficial. While she takes pride in presenting a loving relationship with little or no conflict in it to the outside world, she secretly knows that it is the superficiality that keeps them both safe and their relationship easy. The cost is that they really don't know each other intimately—they don't communicate, they don't grow as people and as a couple, and they don't experience deep love. And because of this, they are ill equipped to deal with a life crisis like the one they're dealing with now. No wonder things are falling apart.

Sophie picks their son up from school and takes him to a friend's home. She asks the friend if she can leave her son there for the afternoon. Sophie kisses her son good-bye and heads home. She knows that the time has come for her and Kevin to face the truth about each other.

Second Step: Communication and Connection

By the time Sophie arrives back home, Kevin has slowly pulled himself together and has begun to finish folding the laundry that Sophie started earlier that day. As Sophie walks into the laundry room, she sees the pain and remorse in Kevin's eyes. She sees that he has been crying. Kevin turns to Sophie and is surprised to see a new kind of strength in the way she carries herself. He doesn't see the usual anxiousness and fuss in her demeanor. After a moment of silence, Sophie speaks first.

"I'm sorry things got so out of hand, and I'm sorry for saying such hurtful things."

"I'm the one who needs to apologize. I took all my problems out on you, and you didn't deserve any of it. The truth is I'm scared."

"I know. I think we're both scared. The future is uncertain."

"Yeah, I understand. But I'm not just worried about our finances. I'm scared that I'm just plain inadequate."

"In what way?"

"As a husband, a father, a man for that matter. This layoff has shaken me to my core. I can't help but believe that somehow I've failed you. For the first time, I have no control over keeping my family safe and secure."

"You haven't failed us, but I can understand why you feel that way. I really can understand the feeling of having no control. I've been feeling the same way."

"Well, I can't help but think that I'm a complete failure and a fraud. Maybe I'm just not the businessman I thought I was. To be honest, I think my biggest fear is that you'll eventually figure out I'm not the man you thought I was and leave me for someone better. Maybe you don't need me at all. You seem to be taking care of business quite nicely on your own. Who knows? Maybe you'd be better off without me."

Sophie sits silently for a few minutes and then replies, "I can understand why losing your job would trigger all those things. I understand how bad you feel. All I was trying to do was help support you and let you know that I loved you and believed in you. When you shut me out, I felt like you didn't think I had anything to offer. I felt utterly helpless. I realize that my role has always been to make you feel like a success, and when I wasn't able to do that, I didn't know what else to do. I'm not sure who I am to you. I'm not sure of my value. I'm so busy hiding behind other people's needs that I'm not sure who I am and what I'm truly capable of."

Kevin lets out a big sigh. He's starting to feel more at ease.

"I'm sorry I shut you out. I just couldn't deal with the fuss. I needed to focus on finding work and keeping it together. There really was nothing you could do to make me feel better. The more you tried to reassure me, the more I felt like a failure. Seeing that advertisement of yours just freaked me out. It was like you were shouting out to the world 'See, my husband is a failure. I need to save my family.'"

Sophie's heart opens and she gently responds. "I understand that's how you feel and it makes sense that being laid off would make you feel insecure. But please know I don't see you as a failure. You are a wonderful man, a good husband and father. I just couldn't tolerate not doing anything. I couldn't tolerate feeling like a nothing. And I guess, secretly, I was scared that you wouldn't be able to find work soon enough. I needed to do something to take care of my own anxieties about not knowing what would happen next. I also needed to feel like a partner, not a child. When you rejected my support, I felt I had no choice but to take care of myself, and honestly, doing so made me feel pretty good. I'm beginning to feel a lot better about who I am as a person in my own right than I have in a very long time."

"Wow. I don't know whether to feel happy for you or more of a mess. I'm glad you're doing something that makes you feel good, but I can't help but wonder where this leaves us. I'm used to being the man of the house, the one that has it together and takes care of things. I like you taking care of me and our son. I certainly don't want you to be the breadwinner. I don't know where we go from here."

"I don't think we can go back to the way things were. I don't want to feel like my only job is to reassure you and help you feel in control. I like the new me."

Kevin starts to feel his muscles tighten. His breath quickens. He feels his anxiety return. He says, irritably, "Look, I don't need you to reassure me. I'm not a child either. I'm not suggesting that you can't pursue your own side business. But I'm still the one that needs to bring in the money. We can't live off of your part-time job. So while it's great that you are enjoying your pursuits, it's still me that keeps our lives going."

"Kevin, please don't get defensive. I'm not suggesting that you're no longer the man of the house. I understand how important it is for you to find a new job. But please don't belittle what I have to offer. That's where I draw the line."

"Let's not start another argument. I'm going to send out some more resumes. Why don't we talk about this more later?"

Days pass and while the silence was broken between Kevin and Sophie, things are still not the same. Something has changed between them. Sophie continues to market her new business. She fusses less about keeping the household looking perfect and takes more time to do the things she enjoys. Kevin still actively looks for employment. He wants to support Sophie in her new business but still finds it difficult to ask her how things are going. Sophie wants to support Kevin in his job search but is also hesitant to bring up a painful and sensitive subject.

In the week following their honest confrontation, Sophie and Kevin try to go about their lives. Kevin can't help but think about all the things Sophie said. He understands that things have to change. He's aware they already have. Regardless, he still fights his resistance to any changes in their marriage. He's not sure what to do next.

Sophie spends time reading self-help books that address marital crises and change. She writes in her journal, expressing her desires and fears in private. She imagines all the different outcomes to her current dilemma with Kevin. She knows she needs to take the lead in order for their marriage to transform into something different—something that will be better than what it was. A marriage in which there is partnership and mutual respect.

Third Step: Understanding and Accepting Each Other

One night while Sophie is reading her self-help book in bed, Kevin comes in to join her.

"So have you found any answers in that book yet?"

"As a matter of fact I've learned some valuable things," Sophie responds playfully.

"Like what? Please, enlighten me," Kevin says in the same playful tone.

"I've learned that couples can fall into a 'codependent' rhythm really easily where each person does things to assuage the other's anxieties. This often happens when one or both of them are scared to deal with their own pain. So instead they focus on the other person, working hard to create an illusion of control. I think we both do this. I think I've avoided taking risks by focusing on your success and well-being instead of my own."

"Hmm, that's interesting. I'll have to think about that more. I do know you spend a lot of energy making sure things are in order. I appreciate that. Maybe I have depended on you to keep things in order more than I should. I do like having control. Maybe I need to be more tolerant."

"I don't mind keeping an orderly home, but I don't want the pressure of feeling like it's my job to make sure you feel in control. I need to focus less on what builds your self-esteem and more on what builds mine."

"I'm okay with that. I want you to feel good about yourself. I understand that I may need to deal with having less control. If losing my job doesn't teach me that, nothing will. Believe me, I've had to come to terms with a lot of things about myself that I'd rather not."

"Hopefully, this whole ordeal will bring us closer. I really would like us to talk more about these kinds of things. I want us to be more open and honest about what's *really* going on. That way, we can support each other and create a more equal partnership."

Kevin takes Sophie into his arms and says, "I want you to be my partner. I don't know how good I'll be at sharing my feelings, but I'm willing to try."

"Thanks, that's all I can ask for. As I read more about this stuff, I'll share the ideas with you. Maybe we can use this book as a guide on how to make things better between us."

With that, Kevin and Sophie turn off the lights and make love for the first time in weeks.

The next day, Kevin feels some lightness in his chest. For the first time since being laid off, he feels optimistic. During the next week, Kevin's curiosity grows and he starts reading Sophie's book on his own. He's surprised at how much he identifies with the concepts. While he absorbs the ideas presented, something shifts. He feels the noose around his resistance loosen. He starts to consider that their marriage could be based on something more. He starts to see Sophie differently, like a real partner he can truly trust and lean on without feeling like a pathetic loser.

"Maybe there is something good that will come out of all this," Kevin says one evening as he and Sophie begin their new ritual of talking in bed before going to sleep.

Sophie's confidence in herself and her husband grows. She says, "I want us to see each other as equals, in this together, knowing that when one person is down, the other is there to pick up the slack and vice versa. I want us to be able to talk about everything, even those things that we don't like about ourselves or believe the other person won't accept."

"I agree. I need to face my fears and doubts and I need to support you more in being and doing what makes you feel valuable."

"I love you," Sophie says as she reaches over and hugs Kevin with a deeper sense of love than she has ever experienced before.

"I love you too." Kevin feels an enormous sense of relief. As he holds Sophie in his arms, he knows everything will be all right. He feels loved and accepted by his wife and appreciates her in a way unlike he has ever experienced before.

This is the beginning of a new relationship for Kevin and Sophie.

Over the next several weeks, they continue to talk about how they will handle their finances. Kevin works hard at securing new employment. Sophie begins to increase her customer base and make more money. Although it's not nearly enough to cover their bills, Sophie feels better about herself and her ability to contribute to the family in new ways. Every time Kevin or Sophie feels anxious about the future, they agree to let each other know. When self-doubts surface, they share them honestly rather than retreating or blaming the other for how they feel. The process is not easy. It is never easy to be that honest with yourself and your partner. It takes time to get comfortable with being vulnerable. Kevin and Sophie's current circumstances have naturally created a lot of anxiety, but they are committed to keeping their communication open and real. They work on solving problems together and have begun to develop a deeper understanding, respect, and love for each other.

Their journey is not without bumps in the road, but their relationship has successfully moved into phase three. They've developed an open, authentic intimate relationship where real love makes anything possible.

The Gifts Available in Phase Three: Transformation and Transcendence

Moving into phase three does more than create deeper intimacy and love between partners. In this phase, personal growth and transformation occur. Something miraculous happens when we are present with what we are truly thinking, doing, and feeling, and when we share those insights with another who listens with compassion, understanding, acceptance, and love. Something shifts. Belief systems that no longer work for us are weakened. Fear and anxiety dissipate. An opening occurs from which we can create more power in our lives—power to think differently about ourselves and our world, power to be truly free to take action from choice as opposed to reactivity, and freedom to love in deep and profound ways.

Kevin and Sophie both experienced transformation. A major family crisis became an opportunity for growth. Both Kevin and Sophie deserve a lot of credit. Not everyone survives a crisis and becomes better because of it. Some people get through the crisis but revert back to business as usual in the aftermath. Relationships can provide a powerful mechanism from which to grow and expand both individually and as a couple.

Let's take a look at what became available to Kevin and Sophie from having gone through this experience together.

Kevin's Self-Discovery and Transformation

Kevin has always worked hard to get others to respect and admire him. He has been able to look quite good most of his life and chose a wife who would also work hard to help him feel and look like a success. During this crisis, he is forced to remove the façade and expose his true beliefs and fears about himself as a man.

In the quiet space of surrender, Kevin confronts his biggest fear—that he simply is not good enough. Not good enough to keep his family secure, not good enough to have a successful career, not good enough to be really loved and accepted by his wife. He knows deep down that these anxieties have been plaguing him for a very long time, probably since his boyhood, when it seemed to Kevin that love and approval were conditional upon doing a good job and looking good to those outside the family.

He understands that his need for order and control is how he keeps up the appearance of doing things right and looking good to others. He begins to understand that while doing so works pretty well most of the time, it takes an enormous amount of energy as well as a toll on his relationships. He maintains his obsession with keeping up appearances at the expense of allowing others, including himself, to be who they truly are.

However, when Kevin gets laid off, his defense mechanisms are no longer enough to keep his fears at bay. He realizes just how tired he is—tired of his unending pursuit of approval, tired of running from his fears. As he allows these revelations to seep in, and releases the struggle against them, something begins to shift. His self-discovery is palpable. He feels a new kind of freedom. However, the real transformation occurs when he shares himself in an incredibly authentic and vulnerable way with his wife Sophie. The authentic sharing of himself moves the transformative process forward because when he hears himself speak his truth, new truths begin to emerge. He starts to consider other possibilities. Maybe he is good enough; maybe he is lovable even with his imperfections. Maybe it's okay not to look so good to everyone after all. Maybe he can manage his own anxieties and allow his wife the space to do other things with her energy.

As he shares his thoughts and feelings with Sophie, he realizes that she really does love and accept him as is. Her compassionate listening helps him accept those things about himself that are so hard to face. Her acceptance and understanding allows Kevin to feel safe, enabling him to share himself in a new way that results in experiencing more love than he has ever felt before—not only love for his wife, but the kind of love that makes one see the world in a different way, that makes one feel anything is possible, and that makes one fearless. Kevin has a transformative experience. He knows that he will never be the same. He has faced his fears and won. He has gained real power in his life. It is through the experience of having to give up control (including the illusion of having control in the first place) that Kevin ironically acquires more power to make conscious choices about his life.

In the months that follow, Kevin reevaluates what he wants to do with his career, how he and Sophie want to share parenting and household responsibilities, and what values are most important. As corny as it sounds, years from now, Kevin will feel that being laid off was one of the best things that ever happened to him.

Sophie's Self-Discovery and Transformation

Sophie is very feeling-oriented. She can sense others' feelings easily and learned early on to do whatever is needed to make the other person feel okay. For the most part, she does this unconsciously. She rationalizes and justifies putting other people's needs before hers with ease. Her motto is "if you're happy, then I'm happy," so it comes naturally for her to do this with Kevin. She puts her dreams on hold and her emotional needs aside so that she can keep her husband happy and free from angst. She feels it is her calling in life and she does it well. She ignores the nagging depression she feels deep down. She focuses on being a good wife and mother, and this has worked well up until the day Kevin was laid off.

Sophie soon realizes that this time she will not be able to contain her husband's anxieties and keep things under control. She's shocked when Kevin rejects her attempts at doing so. The role she has come to depend on to keep her own unmet needs at bay has abandoned her. She is well aware of how helpless she feels. Sophie quickly comes to grips with what her role has been and feels utterly useless when she can't play that role. For the first time, Sophie feels her depression calling. She feels useless, unappreciated, and rejected. And there is nothing she can do. Or is there?

As Sophie comes to grips with feeling the pain and depression that accompanies her current circumstances, she begins to ask herself some questions. She questions if she really wants her role in the family to be what it has always been. She questions how wise it has been to try to manage her husband's feelings at the expense of her own. Slowly, Sophie's depression turns into anger—anger at her husband for shutting her out and taking her job away, and anger at herself for playing it safe. She becomes aware of how limiting her beliefs are about her role as a wife, mother, and woman. She realizes that she does not see herself as an equal to Kevin and secretly blames him for how she feels about herself and her life. As hard as it is, she admits that she doesn't take full responsibility for her own well-being. She has hid behind feeling responsible for her husband's well-being, and she now understands that she had no control over it in the first place.

Sophie feels as if her life is a lie. Her marriage is full of pretenses. She has worked hard to control things that are completely out of her control and *not* her responsibility anyways. Furthermore, she secretly blames others for her failure in being all that she truly can and wants to be. Sophie's anger gives her strength and helps her move into action. She knows that things have to change.

Sophie's transformation begins before she and Kevin ever exchange words. With determination to make a change despite anxiety about doing so, Sophie begins to take risks and do things that reflect her strength, intelligence, and perseverance. She begins to take herself more seriously and focuses on what she does have control over. She works on building her business and taking responsibility for her own emotions and needs, abandoning the role of caring for others at her expense. As she does, Sophie's confidence strengthens. She begins to see a new life for herself, one in which she creates her own value rather than depending on others to create that for her. She visualizes herself having a successful business. Sophie begins to carry herself in a new way, reflecting the new identity that is forming inside her. She's very aware that she no longer wants to live a lie and that her relationship with herself and her family needs to change.

Sophie wants to be seen and treated as an equal partner in her marriage. She wants to feel more like a businesswoman and not solely a housewife and mother. She wants to contribute to her family in multifaceted ways. Sophie begins to establish clearer boundaries. She takes responsibility for her own feelings and needs and insists others do the same. Sophie feels more determination than ever.

She decides to talk to Kevin and let him know that she is no longer willing to be seen as a second class citizen. She knows this is a make or break moment. But when Sophie walks in the door on that fateful day and sees the defeated and vulnerable look on Kevin's face, her plan of attack ceases. She feels compassion and love for him and immediately understands that the game has already changed. She never expects the conversation to go as it did.

Sophie realizes that Kevin has had insights and breakthroughs of his own. She listens with the desire to understand. The more Kevin offers himself to her in an honest and vulnerable manner, the more Sophie understands and admires her husband. She in turn is moved to express her own self-discoveries in a truthful manner as opposed to the aggressive manner she envisioned as she was driving home. The conversation evolves organically. She learns more about Kevin than she thought possible. She shares more about herself than she had intended. In the end, Sophie experiences Kevin in a new way. She holds herself with a new presence. Together, they discover a bond and love unlike any they have experienced before.

Phase Three Lives On

In phase two, self-discovery is the name of the game—a valuable achievement in and of itself. For without self-discovery, the possibilities for growth and change do not exist. In phase three, transformation and transcending one's circumstance is the new game. Self-discoveries turn into possibilities, possibilities drive transformation, and transformation creates deep and profound love (or vice versa; it works both ways).

Kevin and Sophie won the jackpot. They both did the work of reflecting, observing, and questioning their thoughts, feelings, and behaviors. In doing so, they became conscious of what was going on within, and were able to distinguish it from outside pressures. To their credit, they were both able to take the risk of sharing their truths with each other. This allowed them to grow, create more authentic love, and experience more freedom and power. Not a bad return on their investment.

In summary, phase three is really about

- Becoming more proficient at managing your reactions; seeking self-understanding as opposed to blaming

- Inquiring more about who your partner is and your partners intentions

- Accepting your partner for who your partner is, not who you want or fear him to be

- Communicating openly and honestly, sharing yourself authentically

- Making requests, not demands

- Appreciating the mirroring that continually takes place in your relationships; seeing conflict as an opportunity for deeper understanding, acceptance, and love

- Supporting your and your partner's growth and transformation, thus promoting powerful choices in how you want to live your lives

Here's the thing about phase three that you need to know. Most couples never make it to phase three. Those couples that do find it difficult to remain there. Because of the defense mechanisms we have developed, we are hardwired and socialized to live in phases one and two. These defense mechanisms both protect us and hinder us. They protect us from emotional and psychological pain. They hinder us from growth and transformation. Relationships offer us the *opportunity* to grow, but the choice of whether to grow or not is ours and ours alone.

Herein lies your challenge. Know that you will naturally move back and forth from phase one *(being relatively unconscious and lacking any true power)* to phase two *(becoming conscious and having more freedom)* to phase three *(creating real intimacy, love, and transformation)*. This is completely normal. However, the more you practice the skills and tasks needed in phase three, the easier it gets to remain there for longer periods of time. The more you can hang out in phase three, the more love and freedom you will embody.

Again, there is no right way to be. Some couples will naturally move into phase three and enjoy the journey as well as the rewards. Other couples will struggle more. Still others will choose to remain in phases one and two. Whatever you choose is just fine.

However, you can only choose for yourself. If you would like to create more intimacy in your relationship than your significant other, you will need to either accept what is and stay or accept what is and go. When two people stay in different phases, the relationship becomes out of sync. I believe this is one of the primary reasons why relationships end. Relationships tend to last when both people are interested and able to move through the same phases. When there is a significant difference over a long period of time, relationships suffer because the needs and wants of each person become too disparate.

Phase four is a bit paradoxical. While couples define and redefine their relationship from beginning to end, they usually do so from the perspective of a transactional relationship. For example, couples may define their relationship as a means to create a home, raise a family, build careers, maintain everyday responsibilities, and so on. The essence of phase four as defined within our discussion enables a couple to create a relationship that is transformative in and of itself. In other words, the relationship becomes a living, breathing entity, not solely the sum of two parts (individuals). From this context, the relationship's purpose goes beyond transactional functions. Its purpose is to grow and transform, thus impacting not only those that make up the relationship but those that live in the greater community. Good role models are hard to come by, but examples of these relationships might include Ronald and Nancy Reagan, Barack and Michelle Obama, Paul Newman and Joanne Woodward, and Jessica Tandy and Hume Cronyn. You may personally know couples that clearly have transformative relationships. They are hard to describe, but you know that they see their relationship as something to nurture and protect, rather than something that is supposed to nurture and protect them. Their purpose goes beyond themselves. They are held together by love, not fear. They are a powerful and electric force.

Rather than continue to talk about phase four conceptually, let's see how a couple grapples with the challenges and opportunities that phase four presents. I want to introduce you to Claire and Ralph.[1]

---

1. Please note that while we are exploring phase four through the lens of a long-term marriage, couples (married or not) can create relational transformation at any time under varying circumstances throughout their lives.

Phase Four:
Relational Transformation

Claire and Ralph: A Historical Overview

laire and Ralph have been married for 30 years. They have three children, ages 28, 26, and 21. They met in college 33 years ago when Claire was 19 and Ralph 21. They fell in love and dated for a couple of years. Then Claire became pregnant. Claire was raised Catholic and Ralph Jewish. Based on Claire's religious upbringing, marriage was a fairly obvious next step, and they knew that their parents would insist on marriage anyway. Despite their young age and the pressure the pregnancy put on them, Claire and Ralph married three months later, before the pregnancy showed. While both their parents had strong feelings and concerns about the difference in religions, Claire and Ralph were sure they could work things out. Neither one was willing to convert to the other's religion, so they decided they would expose their children to both. While their parents eventually accepted this compromise, neither family was particularly happy.

Ralph's parents and Claire's parents helped support them in the early years. Ralph completed college and then earned a law degree. Claire eventually graduated from college with a bachelor's degree in business, having taken time off to raise their young son. They lived close to Claire's family, who played a very active role in their family life. Ralph's family lived on the other side of the country but did their best to visit often and remain involved in his life. Their second child also came as a surprise. They now had the stress and challenge of raising two children while trying to establish their professional lives. Claire left her first job after their second child was born. After their second child turned two, Claire returned to work in an entry level position in the marketing department of a Fortune 500 company. Ralph passed the bar exam and joined a large law firm to work in their litigation department. Although they both held full-time jobs, Claire and Ralph quickly adopted traditional roles within the family. When they had their third child some years later, they decided that their family was complete. They both agreed that creating a secure home in which to raise their children was their top priority.

In the beginning of their marriage, they struggled to balance the demands of parenting with the demands of forming identities as young adults. As the years passed and their responsibilities grew, they worked hard to meet the large demands on their time and energy. As with most families, they discovered that as two working parents, their internal and external resources were often insufficient to meet all the demands of their three children. Their arguments and conflicts were based primarily on this deficiency. These types of conflicts are typical for couples dealing with multiple demands. Claire felt Ralph did not help out enough with household responsibilities and was resentful that, when one of the kids got sick, he automatically assumed that she would stay home from work. She believed that her career was just as important as Ralph's, although balancing work and family proved stressful and challenging for them both.

Ralph was resentful that their family life revolved so much around Claire's family and church and felt that his values and religious beliefs were pushed aside. He was raised in a family in which traditional roles were the norm and secretly resented Claire's need to put so much time and energy into her work. Ralph felt he made enough money for Claire to stay at home, and from time to time would suggest to Claire that she quit her job to take care of the kids full time. Claire enjoyed having a career and refused to stop working.

The tension between Ralph's needs and expectations and Claire's needs and expectations rose and fell intermittently throughout their marriage. They both had fairly good communication skills and would talk things through when the tension became too great. They problem-solved effectively, usually finding a compromise they could both live with. Their approach was transactional in nature, although they were quite respectful and honest with each other during the process.

Their relationship teetered between phase two and phase three. For the most part, they accepted each other for who they were and shared their thoughts and feelings authentically. However, at times they remained stuck in the power struggle of competing for needs, resources, and the right to be right. Their problem solving remained at a transactional level, resulting in compromises and a tit-for-tat approach. Sometimes they could own their own reactivity and identify their issues. Other times they remained unconscious and unwilling to see what the other person was mirroring. Overall, they had a respectful marriage in which intimacy came and went depending on the current stressors and personal challenges that existed in their lives.

The primary glue that held the marriage together was their commitment to their children. While their religious upbringings were different, the underlying values of family were the same. Ralph and Claire did love each other, although that love varied in intensity over the years. Like all long-term marriages, there were good times and bad. But through it all, the commitment they had to each other and a general mutual liking carried them through the years.

They each had their own support system to turn to when the other was unavailable and had a fairly good balance between independence and dependence with each other, with an emphasis on independence. Both Ralph and Claire got a lot from their careers as well as the family. Family time was how they connected with each other, as they had developed separate interests and friends over the years. Ralph enjoyed professional sports, played golf, and developed a hobby playing poker. Claire enjoyed going to amusement parks with the kids, but when she was with her friends, as she preferred to go out drinking or to comedy clubs.

As the kids got older, Ralph spent more and more time playing poker, getting to the point where he was actually making money at it as opposed to losing. Claire worked long hours but would have fun out on the town with her friends a few times a month. Ralph and Claire made time for each other when the opportunity permitted itself but did not make it a priority. Their need for time together was not that high, and as their needs were fairly compatible in this area, they had little tension over it. Most of their time together was with their children as a family, which they both enjoyed. As their children grew into young adults, Ralph and Claire spent less time together as a couple and family. Neither one complained because they had both developed full lives outside of the family unit over the years and were content to spend most of their time apart.

A New Chapter Emerges: Redefining Their Relationship Once Again

A big change is now occurring in their lives. Their youngest daughter is graduating from college and planning on moving out of the house and into an apartment with her best friend on the other side of town. She is the last child to move out on her own, their two oldest children having moved out and established their own homes some years back. As their daughter's moving day approaches, Ralph and Claire begin to argue more than usual. Sometimes the arguments revolve around how much financial help they should offer their young daughter starting out and other times around old issues that have not surfaced for years, such as who will do the grocery shopping, how much time Ralph is spending with poker games, and how much wine Claire drinks each week.

They continue to bicker until moving day. As they finish helping their daughter unload the last box from the truck, they both give her a big hug and say good-bye. Claire starts to cry. Ralph makes a joke, reminding Claire that their daughter lives only 25 minutes away and she'll probably see her tomorrow when she stops by to do some laundry. The tension is broken, and Ralph and Claire get back into the truck and drive home. The bickering that they had become accustomed to in the weeks prior has turned to silence. In fact, they don't say a word the entire way home.

When they arrive home, Claire goes into her daughter's bedroom, which now contains only some miscellaneous furniture and a couple of pictures hanging on the wall. The house, that had at one time felt so warm and full of life, now feels cold and bare. Ralph goes into his office, turns on the computer, and begins to play poker with his online community. Claire tries to imagine turning their youngest daughter's room into a guest room or a workout room but can't picture it in her mind. She walks out of her daughter's bedroom and down the hall. She passes her son's old room, which had long ago been converted into an office for Ralph, and sees him on the computer playing poker.

She pauses at the doorway, feeling the same coldness and emptiness that she had felt a few moments before. She thinks there is no way the space can be filled. These thoughts settle in her mind as she watches her husband. Without any children at home to fill the space, Claire fears that the abyss between her and Ralph will never be bridged. She watches Ralph for some time, lost in her thoughts. After a few minutes, Ralph notices Claire. "Is there something wrong?" Ralph asks. She replies "No, nothing is wrong. I'm going to go to the gym."

Claire goes to the gym and returns home feeling a little less disoriented. She showers and joins Ralph in their bedroom, where he is watching television. Claire begins to talk. Without knowing it, Claire and Ralph are about to enter phase four.

Ralph and Claire Engage in the Work of Phase Four

Claire tells Ralph how she felt after dropping off their daughter.

"I went into Suzie's room and realized just how empty this house feels without her. And when I was at the gym, I began to think about us and how much of our conversations and interactions have become centered solely on our children. I'm not sure what's left between us when you take the kids out of the mix."

"Well, I don't think things will change that much," Ralph said. "You and I both have demanding jobs. That isn't going to change in the near future. We have interests and friends that occupy our time, we manage to take care of everyday responsibilities, and for the most part we get along. I'm not sure what you're so worried about."

"I'm worried that when I saw you sitting at your desk this afternoon, I felt nothing."

"What do you mean?"

"I mean that I didn't feel connected. It was like our marriage felt as cold and empty as Suzie's room. I feel without anyone else in the house, we will become like roommates, two people that occupy the same space but have little in common and little interest in each other with the exception of making sure the common household responsibilities get taken care of. And I'm not so sure what to make of it."

"I think we settled into a certain rhythm many years ago when the kids got older. I know that we have lost our passion for each other, but I also know that we both basically respect and like each other. For me, at this point, I don't know what I want us to be. I don't know if I have the energy to be anything other than what we are. Work and poker take a lot of my time and energy. You're busy with work and seem to prefer the company of your friends over me, and I've come to accept that."

"I'm just not sure why we're still together, and if it makes sense to pretend there's a marriage when I'm beginning to feel like there may not be. I just don't know what the point is."

"I'm not sure what you're saying Claire but I know it's been a very long day. An emotional one at that, and I think you'll feel better about everything after a good night's sleep. We're not going to solve this tonight, so why don't we just get some rest and resume this conversation another time."

Claire agrees, and Ralph turns off the television and the lights. Claire rolls away from Ralph and, after a while, falls asleep.

Let's stop and take a look at what we know:

1. Ralph and Claire are dealing with the "empty nest" syndrome, a normal and expected part of a long-term marriage that occurs when couples need to redefine their relationship

once children have separated and individuated from them.

2. Their last child leaving home triggered the most current need to revisit and create a new purpose and meaning for their relationship. While there are normal milestones within the life cycle of a long-term marriage that trigger certain issues, facing and dealing with phase four tasks can take place at any time and will most probably occur multiple times throughout a long-term relationship.

3. Ralph and Claire have the experience and skills of communicating honestly and authentically with each other. Their relationship has been built on the ability to successfully resolve issues in phases one, two, and three.

4. Although their marriage has been primarily transactional in nature and its purpose has been defined through their roles as parents, they have been able to create moments of intimacy, acceptance, and love.

5. They have had their share of conflicts, primarily around conflicting needs and desires. They have resolved these conflicts fairly well but in the end created a marriage in which they got most of their personal needs met through activities and people outside the marriage. Most of their needs that got met within the marriage usually involved their children.

6. However, since they started their marriage because of a pregnancy and have been going full steam ever since, Claire and Ralph never had time to establish a relationship without children. Having married at such a young age, neither one had fully individuated as adults. Their marriage has been based on struggling to develop an identity, get their individual needs met, and negotiate the demands of raising three children.

7. The questions that they now have to address include: (i) Now that our primary roles with each other are no longer around parenting

issues, how do we want to reconnect? (ii) Is there enough here to keep us together? (iii) What have we learned from raising a family? (iv) Why did we get married, and do the reasons we married still apply? (v) Who are we now as individuals compared with who we were when we originally fell in love? and (vi) Can we find a new meaning for being together or is our shared history enough?

Let's see what answers await them.

Facing the Honest Truths: Finding New Meaning and Purpose to Their Relationship

Claire and Ralph begin grappling with how and if they want to redefine the purpose and meaning of their relationship. After that initial conversation, Claire and Ralph begin to contemplate living their lives together. While sitting in his office at work one afternoon, Ralph looks back on his marriage. He revisits all the things that he resented—how much time his wife devoted to her career, how Claire and her family took over in terms of raising their children Catholic as opposed to Jewish, how his needs for more passion and freedom were lost at such a young age. He feels like he understands who Claire is and over the years has come to accept the good with the bad.

He remembers how he loved her free spirit when they met and how she loved to have fun and "go for it" despite the tight reins her parents had on her. He respects her determination, while at times he feels like his wants were sacrificed more than hers. He learned many years ago to find other ways to get them met, channeling them into golf and poker, where he feels fully in control. He silently and guiltily remembers the couple of times he was unfaithful when out of town on business but is grateful Claire never found out.

Overall, Ralph concludes that over the years they have found a way to be together that works well enough. The passion may have left, but they have raised three wonderful children, work fairly well as partners in life and give each other the space they need to pursue their separate interests. Ralph doesn't have the energy or enthusiasm to start something new from scratch with another woman. Although he certainly has fantasies about attractive women he meets, he does not see himself as savvy or adventurous enough to pursue those options. Living with Claire is all he knows. He simply cannot see himself living any other life. And while at times this makes him feel empty and depressed, it also gives him a strong sense of security.

Claire and Ralph meet their son and his girlfriend for dinner a few weeks later. As they engage in small talk about the local news, Claire finds her thoughts wandering to the future. What kind of life does she want to have now that their youngest daughter has left the nest? Does Ralph fit into that picture? Is there enough love left between them to survive this shift? She knows that she and Ralph are not the same people they thought they were when they fell in love so many years ago. How young they were and how little they knew. She is amazed at how quickly the past 30 years have gone by. A lot of life has been lived. She is proud of her three children and grateful that her marriage has endured. But now, as she looks across the room at her husband, she wonders who he really is to her. She longs for passion and excitement. She wonders if she can ever have that with Ralph. Claire feels like a big chapter in her life is closing and a new, bigger chapter in her life is opening. She just doesn't know what it is or if it includes her marriage to Ralph.

On the way home from dinner, Claire starts to fantasize about a new life. The more she fantasizes about a new and exciting chapter, the more that fantasy does not include Ralph. She understands that she married Ralph when she was very young. If she hadn't gotten pregnant, would she have married him or eventually broken up with him? Claire remembers how intimate she had become to a coworker ten years ago and how close they came to having an affair. She wonders what her life would have been like if she had followed through with transitioning the emotional affair into a full physical relationship. She misses the feeling of being in love and feels too young to give up the hope of ever feeling that again. While she loves Ralph, she is no longer in love with him. She prefers to go out with her girlfriends, who are more fun and spontaneous. She just doesn't know if there is enough there without the connection of raising three children.

Two days later, Claire turns to Ralph while they are sitting in their living room and resumes the conversation they have been postponing for almost four weeks.

"I've been thinking about us and want to continue the conversation we started the day Suzie moved out."

"What's on your mind?"

"I just think we need to reassess things and see where we stand. I don't think we should just assume that we'll continue in this marriage as usual. I think we both should consider what we want from here on out and if we can do it together."

"What are you saying? Do you want to divorce?" Ralph looks shocked. "I think we get along really well. I don't see any big problems here."

"No, I'm not saying that at all. I'm just saying that I think we have to be honest with each other about what we want out of the next 20 or 30 years of our lives and how we see each other as part of that."

Claire continues to speak as honestly and gently as possible while sharing her fantasies and dreams for her future. She explains how unconnected she feels with Ralph and, says that while she loves him, she is no longer in love. She expresses her sadness at questioning whether or not she can feel any excitement or passion for Ralph and how she wants that desperately in her life once more.

Ralph feels his anxiety build. "I know that we live fairly independent lives and probably don't spend enough time together having fun. Maybe we can find some new activity or common interests and try to rebuild that part of our relationship. Maybe we can rediscover some passion."

Ralph works hard to get his anxieties under control as he comes to terms with the real threat he hears from Claire. He continues to plead his case by saying, "Claire, I really think you need to consider the ramifications of a divorce. We've been through so much together. We've raised a family and will have grandchildren one day in the not-so-distant future. We have so much history together. We've spent our entire adult lives together. I know that the passion died a long time ago, but I think there's still hope. If nothing else, we can live out our lives just like our parents and our grandparents did. I think we should keep the family together for our children's sake. I know the thought of something or someone new sounds exciting. Believe me, I've had fantasies of my own. But the reality of starting over may not be as great as you think. Things may not be that exciting between us right now, but at least we know each other—our marriage is a known factor and that counts for a lot. I'm willing to work on us. I really would like you to consider doing the same."

Claire listens to Ralph's perspective attentively. She can feel his anxiety rise but chooses to listen rather than respond in a reassuring way. She doesn't want his anxieties to take over her need to say what she needs to say, no matter how hard it is for him to hear. Ralph and Claire continue to exchange feelings and concerns about the future of their relationship for another two hours. It is a heartfelt conversation. Ralph and Claire both listen without getting defensive, although at times it is hard to hear each other's honest truths. They take the time to truly listen and consider what the other wants.

In the end, Ralph lets go of his need to convince Claire to hang in there. He wraps up the conversation by saying, "Claire, I don't want you to stay with me if that is not what you want. If you really feel that our history and all we've been through together is not enough and truly believe that we cannot create more passion and love between us, then I will respect your decision to leave. I think we should both take more time to think about this and talk about it more. This kind of decision deserves a lot of consideration. It's that big."

Claire agrees that the decisions are too important to make quickly. She tells Ralph that she will think about everything he said and agrees they should see how things unfold as time goes on.

The Process Continues: The Outcome Emerges

Claire and Ralph spend the next few months continuing the conversation. Ralph goes so far as to take Claire out to more plays and dinners in hopes that they can reignite the spark that left their relationship so many years ago. Claire continues to hope that she will feel more in love with Ralph as they engage in honest discussions about their heartfelt desires. One day, while gardening together, Ralph and Claire's conversation naturally moves into assessing how things are going in their attempt to reignite their relationship.

They agree that they have become better friends through-out the past few months. Ralph says he feels like he understands Claire much better. Claire lets Ralph know how much she appreciates his honesty and efforts to take her out more often. However, in spite of their mutual respect, they both admit that it is highly unlikely that any passion will get reignited. While they both enjoyed the dinners and plays, they still found they enjoyed their separate interests more and did not find spending more time together all that satisfying.

The time has come to decide if they can find a new meaning and purpose for staying together or make the decision to split. Ralph concluded many months ago that he was not up to starting life anew. He just doesn't have the energy and is content to keep things as they are. He wants to focus on being friends with his wife and see what happens in the years to follow. Claire feels more pulled to leave Ralph and take her chances. Although she is still feeling hesitant, Claire is just about ready to tell Ralph that she wants to see how it feels being on her own. She starts to think about how she will ask for a trial separation.

One day Claire is cleaning out her desk drawer. She comes across the DVD that Ralph had given her for her birthday last year. Ralph had organized and copied all their family videos onto one DVD set. He surprised Claire with the DVD last year. Claire had been so preoccupied at the time that she never sat down and viewed the videos. That night while Ralph is out playing poker, Claire puts the DVD on and spends the next five hours watching her life with Ralph. Claire finds herself smiling, laughing, and even crying as she relives the memories of their life together. She feels her heart expand as she watches her children's birthday parties, graduations, soccer games, and first steps. She feels love in her heart as she is reminded of how great a father Ralph truly was and still is.

Then Claire begins to visualize telling her children that she and their father are separating. She begins to imagine how the holidays will feel. She tries to envision bringing someone new into her life and how that would play out. She thinks about everything Ralph said, such as how much they've been through together. Claire decides that their shared history and sense of family is worth more than her restlessness and need for passion. Creating a family legacy provides stability and resiliency, not only for her and Ralph but for future generations to come. Having come so close to stepping out the door,

Claire now sees herself in her mind's eye close the door, safely retreating back inside.

Claire shares her thoughts with Ralph when he arrives home late that night. Ralph is relieved. He likes the idea of creating a relationship that represents a link from generations past to generations to come. He starts to see himself as the steward of this family legacy. He begins to envision what kind of legacy he and Claire can create. They talk about different ways they can impact their children, grandchildren, and great-grandchildren. They brainstorm ideas on how they can leave the planet a better place for future generations. As they talk into the early hours of the morning, Claire and Ralph begin to feel excited about their future. For the first time in a very long time they have a common purpose that goes beyond simply meeting their parental responsibilities and trying to get their own needs met. This is not a cure all, but it is a very good start.

Let's stop and take a look at what we know:

1. Claire and Ralph's marriage was at risk.

2. Ralph was willing to live with things as is, although "as is" certainly was far from

perfect. Claire was less willing to stay in a relationship that lacked passion and emotional connection.

3. If a greater purpose and meaning to their relationship was not created, then it was highly likely that Claire would have initiated a separation.

4. By seeing her life through the lens of a camera, Claire found a greater purpose and meaning to her marriage that went beyond her individual needs. She decided that their shared history would be enough to hang in there, at least for the time being. She felt a responsibility to her family's past and future. She understood that she was a part of something bigger than herself—her family's legacy. Claire decided she was not willing to throw all that away.

5. As Ralph and Claire continued to talk and create a greater meaning and purpose to their relationship, the vision expanded. They began to see how they could impact

future generations. They began to envision creating a family legacy that not only served their family but other families and communities as well.

6. This process required time, patience, reflection, dialogue, honesty, acceptance, and creativity. In the end, it was their commitment to the relationship that allowed this conclusion to emerge. If their only commitment was in meeting their own individual needs, then the outcome would have been different—not better or worse, just different.

Ralph and Claire have successfully engaged and continue to traverse phase four.

Epilogue: Phase Four Does Not End Here

Claire and Ralph were able to identify a greater meaning and purpose to their relationship that worked at this time in their lives. While their individual needs were not fully met within the marriage, they found something from which to move forward. However, creating the vision is just the beginning. Ralph and Claire will need to be and act in ways that support the vision and bring it to life. In other words, when Ralph makes a decision to play poker or donate money to a cause, he will need to see if these choices are in alignment with the relationship's new purpose and meaning. Claire will need to do the same. She will need to ask herself if her actions and choices are motivated by the relationship's needs or her own needs for ego gratification.

In truth, creating the purpose and meaning for the relationship is the easy part. Acting in alignment with that purpose and meaning is much more challenging. This is where many couples get stuck. It is easy to get caught up with trying to get your own needs met. It is harder to accept that higher needs get met only when the needs of the relationship get met first. It is easy to act from fear and deprivation. When doing so, couples will find themselves regressing back into their transactional way of relating to each other. This is why most relationships do not enter or stay in phase four. It is far more common to define your relationship from a *transactional* point of view rather than a *transformational* point of view.

Although Ralph and Claire have taken on the challenges and opportunities that live in phase four, time will tell how this chapter unfolds. It is certain that they will need to revisit the work of phase four again. There may come a time when this purpose no longer works for them. There may come a time when it simply is not enough.

Many things will change. One day they may retire from their jobs, their children may get married and have children of their own, someone may get ill, other people will come and go, unforeseen events will take place in the world, and one or both may discover they can no longer find meaning and purpose in the relationship and decide to leave. Such is the nature of life. Just as couples go in and out, back and forth, between phases one, two, and three, couples will define and redefine their relationship many times over. For Ralph and Claire, this is not their first encounter with phase four and it most certainly will not be their last.

In summary, phase four is really about

- Relating to your relationship as a living, breathing life force in and of itself

- Creating a shared purpose and meaning for the relationship (that is, a vision)

- Supporting the vision by acting and making choices accordingly

- Understanding that the well-being of the relationship is equally if not more important than the well-being of any one individual within

- Finding ways that further and deepen the purpose and meaning of the relationship

- Taking the time to revisit and redefine the relationship's purpose and meaning as the needs of the relationship change and evolve over time

There are many ways to create meaning and purpose. Every couple will tackle this process in their own way, in their own time. The greater purpose may be creating a haven from which to raise a family, creating a space for making dreams come true, seeking adventure, teaching tolerance or spreading kindness, and so on. What's most important is that the relationship has a purpose, a heartbeat all its own. The relationship itself becomes a living, breathing entity—one to be protected and nurtured, one that creates greatness and comfort, and one that generates selflessness and commitment to the well-being of others.

Summary

We've seen how other couples grapple with the challenges they face as they navigate their relationships through the four phases. While developing relationships takes commitment on our part, the rewards are plentiful.

Let's review what's available to us through our relationships with others.

- We learn about ourselves and get to see our blind spots through the eyes of others.

- We're able to practice tolerance and learn acceptance.

- We learn to distinguish what we know about another from what we are projecting; we understand others more profoundly.

- We get to support others in their own journeys, and receive support for our own.
- We have the opportunity to transform ourselves and our world.
- We learn to love ourselves, express our love for others, experience love, and become love.

I believe that love and transformation are the essence of our lives. Our evolution requires this; our salvation demands it. I have referred to both these concepts throughout this book. In fact, I have gone so far as to suggest that relationships are our primary vehicle for creating love and transformation. As we conclude our discussion, let's reflect on what love and transformation are. Let's take a look at how we might define them and how they apply to the four phases of a developing relationship.

PART THREE

Love and Transformation

People want to be seen, validated, understood, and loved for who they truly are. That's all we need in order to grow and flourish; this is the food for our hearts and souls.

What Is Love?

There are as many thoughts and ideas about what love is as there are people who make the inquiry. Love is one of the primary gifts that one receives from moving through the four phases. The type of love and depth of love shifts and deepens as your relationship continues to develop. My hypothesis is that the further along you are in the development of your relationship, the more intimate and profound love you will experience. If this proves to be the case, then it only makes sense to explore more of what this gift entails. So here goes my attempt to define love. Please remember that this is only a point of view. I am not the holder of any absolute truth in understanding love. I wouldn't dare be that presumptuous or take on that responsibility.

I think it is best to start out with the different forms of love as we know them today. Love is experienced in many ways. Some forms of love will be experienced more so in one phase than another. As I go through them, I will highlight which phases access the different types of love. As I attempt to describe love in varying ways, I may omit an experience that you have had that exemplifies love differently. If this is the case, I welcome your input and have listed ways for you to contact me at the end of this chapter. Remember, we are all unique individuals. We have a common experience specific to being human but, within that context, we each have our own unique experiences.

Let's begin with the most basic expression of love.

Love as hormones includes dopamine, testosterone and oxytocin, all of which produce the feeling of being in love. Dopamine is the attraction hormone. Testosterone and dopamine are what drive us sexually and produce that high feeling. When dopamine is at play, you feel like you're floating on clouds and your new significant other is the next best thing to chocolate pie a la mode. So what does this mean? Does it mean that you're really not in love and only feeling the effects of these powerful hormones?

Does it really matter? Feeling in love is feeling in love no matter what hormone might be at play. And while the heady feeling of being in love is temporary, it is a wonderful phase in relationships. It just needs to be understood so you don't make poor choices. Feeling "in love" can cloud judgment and distort reality. Love as dopamine and testosterone most commonly occurs in phase one, although you can still feel some of its residual effects in other phases. Remember, phase one is when you project the most. It is the time you are most unconscious. It is the phase in which you must be cautious and remain clearheaded enough to get out of a relationship if it is dangerous and unhealthy.

Regardless, feeling in love is so powerful that many people choose to stay in phase one over and over again with different people, or even with the same person, just so that feeling can be sustained. It truly is drug-like. And while it is a wonderful expression of the human biology and spirit, it can be misunderstood. On the flip side, the dopamine effect is what propels procreation and gives us the feeling that we can do anything and that everything is right with the world. It's hard to beat that.

Oxytocin, on the other hand, is the hormone of attachment. This hormone begins to take effect in phase one as well. However, contrary to the other hormones, oxytocin's full effects extend further into the development of the relationship. It takes hold and grows as the relationship progresses into phases two, three, and four. So that you'll understand just how potent this hormone is, oxytocin is what kicks in when a woman gives birth to her baby. It is nature's way of ensuring that mothers attach to their babies and ensure their survival. I remember it happening when my first daughter was born. She was less than 24 hours old when I glanced over at her in the hospital's port-a-crib and it hit me all at once. I fell so in love with her that it almost hurt. I couldn't believe what I was feeling. I had never felt such a powerful emotion in my life. I knew in that moment I would never be the same. My life would never be the same. I was attached to this little new person forever. The bond would never be broken.

While giving birth will stimulate this hormone dramatically and suddenly, oxytocin is produced at other times in both men and women (although women in general have higher levels of oxytocin in their systems).

Regardless as to when, how much, and why this hormone is released, the effects are the same. Love takes on a feeling of attachment. A deep need to protect your loved one develops with the understanding that pain and loss are at stake if that person gets hurt or goes away. Love as hormones has no logic or rationale. In this case, love is not run by our head or even our heart. It is run by our biology, by our hormones. I'm sure we can all remember a time when our hormones got the better of us. Fortunately, we are more than our endocrine (hormonal) system.

In conclusion, the fact that these feelings of love and attachment can be traced to hormonal influences designed to ensure the survival of the species does not diminish the experience of "hormonal" love in any way. As I was looking at my newborn daughter, I could have cared less if oxytocin was at play or not. The experience of love was so profound it still makes me cry just thinking about it. I wouldn't trade it for anything.[1] It is one of nature's best ingredients and enables us to feel love in a wonderful and magical way.

---

1. Although there have been many challenging parental moments when an extra dose of oxytocin wouldn't have hurt.

Love as acts of kindness is another way people define and experience love. This idea suggests that we feel love through our actions. In other words, when we act with kindness and love toward someone, we generate the feeling of love. In this case, we use our actions as both an expression and creation for love. These expressions of love are pure in nature and are extended simply because someone is committed to the well- being of another person at that moment in time. There are no hidden agendas, no manipulations.

When we are moved to act with kindness toward others, we experience love, gratitude, and healing. When we receive acts of kindness from others, we experience the same. The lesson is that giving and receiving acts of kindness has benefits that go far beyond the words or actions extended. Be generous with both.

Love as acts of kindness can be experienced during any phase of a developing relationship, although it is at the heart of the matter in phases two and three. When it comes to romantic love, we tend to expect that our partners will treat us with kindness, with love. As we come to understand the challenges and tasks associated with the developing relationship, it is easy to understand why we often fall short of expressing love through kindness. We are too busy reacting and projecting. We feel hurt and disappointed. Our reactions trigger their reactions, and so on. The wounds deepen and we dig a deeper hole.

Because we get so triggered by our significant others, acting with kindness at all times is challenging. It is through the work of phases two and three that we begin to recognize and manage these reactions, thus creating space for more kindness and understanding. The opportunity to experience more love becomes available to us. As we clear away the junk (our internal *garbage*) in phases two and three, we are able to experience more love by acting accordingly. That is why deeply intimate relationships create deeper experiences of love.

It is important to note that while our discussion is focused around romantic relationships, love exists everywhere. It is available to us at all times. If we are kind to others wherever we go, the amount of love and well-being that we can generate becomes infinite. Imagine a world where everyone is committed to the well-being of others. Imagine a world where we act with kindness first.

Love as a thought is similar to love as an action. When we think loving thoughts, we feel love. It really is as simple as that. There have been many studies and theories that suggest our reality is in large part created by our thoughts. The mind is that powerful. If this is true, or even partially true, then it is logical to conclude that the more loving thoughts we have, the more love we will experience in our lives. Thoughts lead to feelings, feelings lead to actions, and actions lead to impact. The process comes full circle when we interpret the subsequent impact. Depending on how we interpret things, we either reinforce or challenge our original beliefs or thought patterns.

While in theory this all sounds simple enough, in reality changing our thought patterns can be a daunting task. The manner in which we perceive, organize, analyze, and formulate our thoughts is developed early in life and is very reinforcing by its own design. Our mind works through many different mechanisms in a systematic way. Our thought process is influenced by our physiological and neurological makeup, early life experiences, environmental factors, and basic personality structure. Once a neurological pattern is established in the brain, a logical construct is formed. Once this occurs, it is very difficult to break our default method of interpreting events. Our belief system is designed to reinforce itself. It is much easier to perceive things in a way that correlates with our past experiences and beliefs than to alter the neurological patterns in our brain. To make matters worse, this process occurs almost instantaneously. We attach meanings to events so quickly that we are busy reacting to those meanings before we even understand what happened. The good news is that with patience and practice we can alter our thought patterns and create new beliefs.

Love as a thought can be tapped into in all phases of a developing relationship, although it is more easily accomplished in the later stages, after you have mastered the tasks in phases one and two. Remember, your relationships provide an excellent mirror into your thoughts and beliefs. As you observe how you react to others and how others react to you, your default ways of thinking become revealed. In other words, if you believe that people are giving, you will see others as giving and react accordingly. If you believe that people are selfish, you will see others as selfish and react accordingly to that. Your reactions to others are based more on your thoughts and beliefs than you realize.

Keep in mind that in phase one, your significant other is more object than real person. You project all your stuff, both good and bad, onto that person. Phases one and two give us the opportunity to sort all that out. We have the opportunity to test our assumptions and understand what mind-set is at play. When we do this, we are able to manage our thoughts better. Once we begin to manage our thinking patterns and belief systems, we can then make choices. We can eliminate thoughts and beliefs that no longer work for us and create ones that do. We can choose to experience love as a thought. We can choose to think with love.

Love as a feeling is the most common experience we have of love. We can feel love in all phases of the developing relationship although the essence of this feeling may differ from one phase to another. In general, we feel love in our hearts. When we lose someone we love, we refer to our heart as broken. So much of this business we call love is a matter of the heart. While love can fill the entire body, we tend to identify the heart as its core. I can't help but wonder why this is so. The heart's basic function is to pump our blood from one part of the body to another. And yet, most people will point to their hearts when asked where they feel both their love and pain. What is it about this particular organ that gives it the power to hold our love?

I have no scientific explanation for this, although there may be some researcher out there that does. I only know that the "emotional heart" has an uncanny ability to expand and contract beyond measure. Most, if not all, of you have had the experience of feeling your heart expand as it fills with love. Additionally, you may have had the experience of your heart contracting as it contends with loss. Emotional healing seems to occur within our hearts. It will contract to protect itself and expand to transform itself. We seem to know so much about this blood-pumping organ and yet so little when it comes to understanding what portals it holds. The heart is truly a mysterious and wonderful part of our human anatomy.

So what do we know for sure about our feelings? The amygdala is a part of the brain that generates and processes emotions. It is where neurological and hormonal activity is triggered by the brain's interpretation of events. In other words, most feeling states can be traced back to our survival instincts that lie deep within our genetic code. If we perceive an event as threatening, our feelings and actions will follow accordingly. If we perceive an event as life sustaining, our feelings and actions will respond accordingly as well. So while we may feel love or fear in our hearts, those feelings are generated elsewhere. It is fair to say that love as a feeling may be more a function of our biological design than we care to admit.

Where does this lead us? On the one hand, love can be traced to neurological and hormonal processes. On the other hand, there is no doubt about the power of love. Love heals and transforms. Whether you subscribe to the biological understanding of love or the spiritual, heartfelt experience of love, the outcome will be the same. Love as a feeling is all good. It boosts our immune system; it promotes tolerance, understanding, and good will; and it creates more happiness in our lives.

Love as spirit suggests that our true essence, our soul, is nothing more and nothing less than love. For some, this love is called God; for others, it's called life's force, for others, it may be called something else entirely. Regardless of your beliefs, love as spirit implies that this source of love is available anytime, anyplace. It lives within us, is us, and surrounds us all the time.

Love as spirit can be accessed in many ways. Some access it through meditation, others through prayer. Regardless of the approach, when you are able to be truly in the present moment, you are more able to be aware of your connection to love as spirit. Some will suggest that love as spirit is guiding us all the time. Many people believe that love as spirit is the energy from which we are born and to which we will return. Regardless of how you prefer to see the world, love just may be the universal energy that connects us, guides us, and defines us.

Love as spirit is available to us regardless of where we stand in relationships. We are able to experience love because we are love. It is only our minds and past experiences that muddy the waters. When we are able to see ourselves and others for who we truly are and not the projections and distorted beliefs we've created, we are able to experience, even be, profound love. Someone once asked me if I believed in God. I replied by saying that I wasn't sure if God exists. I wasn't sure how I defined God. I was then asked what I believed in, if not God. I replied by saying that while I wasn't sure about my belief in God, I was sure about the power of love. I believe in the collective whole. I know that when a community of people come together in love to make a difference, anything is possible. Maybe this is the place from which we can all gather. Maybe love is the common denominator that will help us tolerate, even celebrate, our differences. Maybe it is not only the place to start, but the place from which we will be saved.

Love as spirit is really love of self. It is not dependent upon another human being. It does not require that you be in any romantic relationship. It does not reflect our biology or mind. It just is. And it is available to you at any time. Remembering who we really are, loving ourselves for who we truly are, is the best thing we have going. It enhances our lives and the lives of others. It is the *Pathway to Ourselves* and the *Pathway to Each Other.*

What Is Transformation?

The one thing in life we can count on is change. Evolution demands it. The laws of nature support it. This fact of life elicits both assurance and anxiety—anxiety for the lack of control and basic uncertainty, assurance in the fact that, "this too, shall pass." On the one hand, human beings struggle with change. We resist. It frightens us. So when our relationships call for change and transformation, we react.

On the other hand, human beings are incredibly resilient and adaptable. We transcend crises and challenges all the time. We change when our circumstances demand this. We transform who we are in order to fulfill our potential. So when our relationships call for change and transformation, we respond.

Change is a tricky business. Sometimes we choose it and sometimes it chooses us. Life keeps coming whether we want it to or not. How we react or respond to change is what really matters. This is the moment when change can become transformative. This is where we always have choice. By choosing transformation we choose power over control, love over fear.

How do we define transformation? I believe transformation can be looked at from two perspectives. The first perspective suggests that you are evolving or changing from one state or way of being to another. You are becoming someone new, different, better. The second suggests that you are returning to, rather than moving toward, your authentic self. This is accomplished by removing all the "clutter" that has accumulated over the years. By removing the layers of distorted beliefs, interpretations, stories, pain, hurt, fear, betrayals, and so forth, from your *inauthentic self,* you are free to once again be your *true self.* Regardless of which perspective resonates, the outcome remains the same. Transformation creates more well-being. Love creates more transformation. Relationships create more love.

Relationships by their very design are the perfect vehicle for transformation. They allow us to experience self-discovery and love. They provide a window into ourselves and a mirror unlike any other. In our relationships we are given the opportunity to not only understand who we are but to take full responsibility for who we are and what we do. When we are fully aware of our thoughts, feelings, and actions, openings for transformation occur. It is in these moments that we are able to change a belief, choose a different response, feel a different emotion, let go of something that no longer works, become a new potential, return to our true selves.

Think back on all the people you have known throughout your lifetime. They have offered you different perspectives at different times. For example, a childhood friend you grew up with may have reflected an aspect of yourself you were not ready to see at the time, let's say your inability to share. Later in life, your college sweetheart may have mirrored that same quality about yourself but in a certain way that allowed you to see that quality more clearly. We call these "insights" or "light bulb moments," and they are the opening into new worlds and ways of being. It is just too hard to see ourselves clearly when living in a vacuum. We need mirrors. We need to act as mirrors for each other. There are always new things to learn and understand. Sometimes we get it and sometimes we don't. Therefore, we are always in need of reminders. Without them, transformation cannot occur. So next time you find yourself reacting to someone or something, say in your mind's eye, "Oh, I get what I need to see. Thank you for reminding me."

Relationships are designed to illuminate and bring out both the best and worst in us. They provide us the opportunity to support one another in our journeys. They encourage us to grow and transform. They generate understanding, acceptance, and love. They are that special. Take care of your relationships. Cherish them, protect them, and nurture them.

> *Why, you ask one more time?*
>
> *Because...*
>
> *We need each other*
>
> *We learn about ourselves through others*
>
> *We need to love and be loved*
>
> *When we are a people committed to the well-being of each other, everyone wins*
>
> *It's time to get Back to Ourselves, Back to Each Other*

What Next?

After people read this book, they always have the same questions. What next? What should I do? What should I be thinking about? I have created a comprehensive step-by-step workbook and guide in order to specifically answer these questions. In the meantime, let me give you some questions to ask yourself as you reflect on how you impact your relationships and how your relationships impact you.

- Am I aware when I am having a strong reaction to my significant other?

- Do I understand what buttons get pushed? Do I understand where those reactions come from?

- Can I separate out the present reality from my past experiences, fantasies, and fears?

- How often do I make myself or my significant other wrong?
- Do I really know my partner's intentions or am I making assumptions?
- Do I take the time to understand my significant other? Do I accept him for who he is, not who I wish he were?
- Do I make concessions in ways that compromise my personal integrity and values?
- Am I able to share myself authentically?
- What kind of relationship do I want? How would I describe that relationship to others?
- Am I willing to put my relationship's needs above my own personal gratification?
- Am I committed to creating more understanding, acceptance, and love?

We are perfectly imperfect human beings. How you answered the questions above and what thoughts came as a result will tell you where you stand today. There are no right or wrong answers. You are on your own unique journey. You alone will need to decide what phase of the developing relationship is challenging you most at this point in time. Remember, different phases will present themselves at different times throughout the lifetime of your relationship. Just because you've been with someone for many years and think you know them inside and out, don't think that issues found in phase one won't pop up again. They will. We are always a work in progress.

Moreover, even though you may have traversed certain phases successfully in one relationship, this doesn't mean that those same tasks will be easily mastered within another relationship. Just as individuals are all unique, so are relationships. There is always something new to learn about yourself. There is always something new to understand about another. There is always something new to create.

And of course, we need to be reminded of this over and over again.

One last thought. It is not easy to navigate all the tasks outlined in the four phases of relationships on your own. The questions I proposed above may be easy to answer yes or no to, but you may find it challenging to figure out how to actually do things differently. In other words, *easier said than done.* So I encourage you to seek support and help when needed. It may be in the form of books, therapists, mentors, clergy, family members, or a multitude of other sources for support and guidance. Whichever method you prefer, don't be afraid to ask for help. You don't need to go at it alone. Remember, we need each other.

Please don't hesitate to reach out to us for continued support and resources at www.JulieOrlov.com.

With that, I wish you the very best.

⌒Julie

julie@JulieOrlov.com

Resources

For more information or to order the following products and services, please go to www.JulieOrlov.com. You will also find weekly tips, our BlogSpot, upcoming events, and all the latest news from Julie Orlov.

Products

The Pathway to Love Workbook and Guide: Create Intimacy and Transform Your Relationships through Self-Discovery

Take your relationship to the next level! This workbook and guide takes you step-by-step through the four phases of your developing relationship. You will get to know yourself and your significant other profoundly. Through the various exercises, you will gain insights that create openings for growth and transformation. Each section allows you to practice and implement the skills and tasks that each phase presents. You will be able to create new ways of relating to yourself and others. This book is your personal guide through the four phases of your developing relationship.

The Pathway to Love: Audio Guide

Listen and learn anytime, anywhere! This Audio Guide includes an overview of the four phases of the developing relationship, along with the tasks and opportunities each phase presents. You will hear real stories from real people who are going through the four phases. You will be able to listen in as Julie Orlov personally guides them through the challenges faced, lessons learned, and successes reached. You will learn what you can do in order to navigate your own journey through the four phases of your developing relationship. This Audio Guide is the perfect tool to help you create more understanding, acceptance, and love in your relationships.

Other Services

Experiential Seminars

There's no better way to learn how to develop your relationship than by exploring the four phases in real-time with others. *The Pathway to Love* Seminars provide an experience in which you can understand the tasks, practice the skills, and integrate new insights and discoveries about yourself, your significant other, and your relationship. This is accomplished through specific exercises, discussions, and group support. The beauty of the seminar's design is that you do not need to come with a partner or currently be in a relationship in order to gain the benefits that this program provides.

Private Coaching

If you and your partner want to work on developing your relationship in a private one-on-one setting, then *The Pathway to Love* coaching program is for you. You will receive eight private sessions designed to enable you to understand which phases you have traversed, how to work with the challenges and opportunities that exist in your relationship, and then define the relationship you want and learn how to get there. The sessions will adhere to the concepts and frameworks presented in *The Pathway to Love* books and are not intended to provide or replace psychotherapy for individuals or couples.

For more information on any of our products or services, please visit www.JulieOrlov.com or e-mail us at support@JulieOrlov.com.

About the Author

Julie Orlov has devoted 24 years to helping people transform their lives through her work as a psychotherapist, executive coach, trainer, speaker, and consultant. While her life's work has taken many paths, she remains passionate about empowering others to create relationships that work. She started her career in clinical social work, treating individuals, couples, and families, expanding her work to leaders and groups so that relationships could thrive in organizations and businesses alike. As a consultant and trainer, she strongly believes in helping leaders develop the capabilities to make a positive difference in the lives of those they lead. She has written and published a variety of articles and has appeared on radio and television. Her vision is to help create a global community in which we are all committed to each other's well-being.

Julie Orlov holds a master's degree in organizational leadership from Chapman University, a master's degree in social work from University of Southern California, and a bachelor's degree in psychology from University of California, Los Angeles. She is a member of the National Association of Social Workers and the American Society of Training and Development, Los Angeles, where she served as the 2010 president on the board of directors. She has also served as foundation chair for KindredSPIRITS, a humanitarian organization located in San Pedro, California.

Julie Orlov currently lives in Southern California with her two lovely daughters, one loyal canine companion, and one temperamental lovebird.

For more information on Julie Orlov, please visit www.JulieOrlov.com.